THE UNICYCLIST,

THE VICAR

AND THE

PAEDIATRICIAN

With best wishes

Pete

THE UNICYCLIST, THE VICAR AND THE PAEDIATRICIAN

Peter and Joseph Sidebotham

Matador
9 Priory Business Park
Kibworth Beauchamp
Leicestershire LE8 0RX, UK
Tel: (+44) 116 279 2299
Fax: (+44) 116 279 2277
Email: books@troubador.co.uk
Web: www.troubador.co.uk/matador

ISBN 978 1780885 155

British Library Cataloguing in Publication Data.
A catalogue record for this book is available from the British Library.

Typeset in 11pt Aldine401 BT Roman by Troubador Publishing Ltd, Leicester, UK

Matador is an imprint of Troubador Publishing Ltd

Printed and bound in the UK by TJ International, Padstow, Cornwall

For Helen

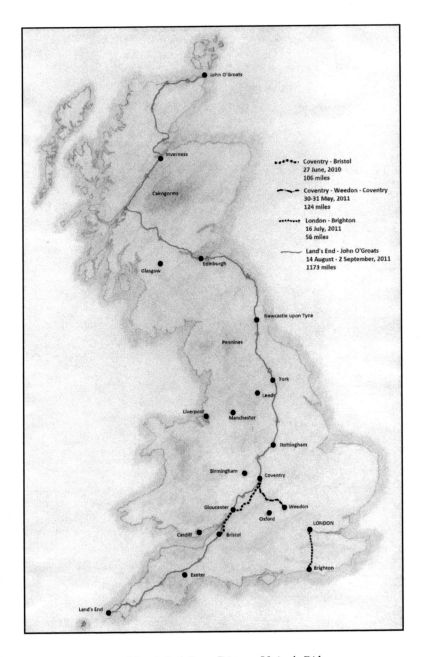

Map 1: Joe's Long Distance Unicycle Rides

PART 1
Coventry to Bristol

PART I

CHAPTER 1

Two guys, three wheels and a dog

I think I somehow missed the first part of the conversation. When I came in, Helen my wife was talking with our son Joe. They seemed to have decided that Joe was going to unicycle from Coventry to Bristol, and that I would accompany him on my bike, riding behind to make sure he was safe on the roads. Not that I object in any way to doing some father-and-son bonding activity. I'm all for that. But I wonder if I might have been given a voice in the choice of activity. I'm not entirely sure whether I was simply out of the kitchen at the time, or whether I was happily washing up with my mind on some higher plane. I enjoy washing up. Joseph doesn't. That's just one of the ways we are different. And I suspect most people would consider me the aberrant one in this discrepancy. But I genuinely do. I find it relaxing; a chance to do something that doesn't require a lot of thought, in which you can take pride in a job well done. I was brought up to view washing up as a sociable activity and one in which everyone helps out. I suspect I did my fair share of grumbling about it in my teenage years, but somehow it stuck. Sadly, this attitude doesn't seem to extend to the rest of the family, so I often end up alone in the kitchen lost in my own thoughts.

So there we were, standing in the kitchen, the washing up half done, and a mad plan involving a lot of hard grind. Meanwhile Esther – Joe's older sister – was sitting in the other room, her back against the radiator to keep warm, stroking Neo our dog, and totally unaware of the momentous venture that was to dominate our lives for the next two years. With the exception of Joseph, all of the family were at that time unaware that this long-distance unicycle ride was in fact nothing more than a warm-up for a much longer ride that was already in his sights.

Coventry to Bristol is about 80 miles as the crow flies. I'm not convinced they do fly in a straight line though, so perhaps that isn't particularly accurate. The AA Route Planner told me it is 103 miles in a car. Of course, we wouldn't have the benefit of the motorway (or a car), so it looked like a bit of planning was in order. The Sustrans National Cycle Route 41 goes between Bristol and Rugby, so covered a reasonable portion of our route. Unfortunately a large section of it between Stratford-on-Avon and Gloucester is merely a proposed route and most of the rest is on-road cycling. Still it provided a good starting point for looking at where we might go. Using this, several Ordnance Survey maps, Multimap, and a road atlas, we managed to enter a more detailed route into the Route Planner. 99.7 miles. So let's call it a round 100 miles. Not bad for a first attempt at long-distance unicycling. One nice thing I discovered looking at the OS maps was that this route is (relatively) flat. It mostly follows the wide Severn valley downstream. This is most important, particularly for a unicycle, as you don't get the wonderful advantage of freewheeling on the downhill sections.

That was also a bit of a bonus for me. I am not an avid cyclist – I do it because it is convenient, quicker than walking, and good for both my health and the environment. I don't do fast though, and I don't see the attraction of Lycra. I would need to go and look at the frame to tell you what make my bicycle is, let alone what model, and talk about brackets, cranks and derailleurs will leave me looking blank. Certainly any prospect of slogging up hills, struggling to breathe, with the sweat pouring down your back, and your legs shouting out at you to stop doesn't appeal.

I am also not a dog lover. Not that Neo is bad as they go: he doesn't slobber, rarely farts, and although he still barks at the doorbell, whines when he wants a walk, smells when he's wet, and leaves muddy footprints on the kitchen floor, he will (mostly) come when he's called, he lies in his cage at mealtimes and isn't too demanding of attention. I say I'm not a dog lover. Most of my friends seem to think this is just a front and that, at heart, I am a closet canophile.

In spite of my reservations about dogs and wheels, it seemed I was stuck with them. So it was that Joe, Neo and I set out along the

Kenilworth Road cycle track on our first practice ride: Joe on one wheel, I on two, and Neo out front on all four paws. Yes, Neo did come with us on that first ride. We had no intention of taking him on our long-distance ride, but he relished the opportunity for a decent run along the cycle track between Coventry and Kenilworth and the disused Crackley railway track.

We struck up a lovely pace cycling along the disused railway, with Neo setting the pace: 20 minutes to do two miles on my later calculations. I forgot to check my watch when we set out from home, but overall it took us around two hours to cover the full 10 miles. Not a great speed – we would need to do a lot better than five miles an hour if we were to cover Coventry to Bristol in one day – but it was a start. There were a few other people out walking dogs or taking younger children for an easy cycle. The sun was low on the horizon to the south-west, with clear blue skies and hints of pink as daylight turned to dusk. The track got a bit muddy towards the end but not enough to hinder our progress. As we came off the railway at Burton Green, Joe took Neo on the extending lead on the pavement while I went along the road, adjusting my pace to theirs. I think Joe only came off his unicycle once as he came up off a crossing, when a kerb unexpectedly dropped down again and Neo was pulling him on to catch up with me. A few grazes when we got home, but nothing major. At least Joseph didn't seem too fazed by the grazes and just remounted and kept on going.

By the time we got back to Canley it was fully dark. Joe decided to go the short way through the woods at Canley Ford. My LED light wasn't quite bright enough to illuminate the track so it made for interesting cycling, and we had to walk up the final section of root-traversed path. We were all a bit muddy by the time we got back home, but it was a great start to our training and a much-loved leg stretch for Neo.

CHAPTER 2

The unicyclist

Hi, I'm Joe. In the summer of 2011 I turned 16, and decided to mark this by cycling from Land's End to John O'Groats – on a Unicycle. This book is the story of that journey and all that led up to it, including my first long-distance unicycle ride from Coventry to Bristol. Well, sort of. When my dad suggested the idea of writing a book, I assumed he meant some kind of story of the journey with the events leading up to it. Of course – this being written by Dad – it was nothing of the sort. It ended up focusing on more obscure subjects, namely our family, washing up, and communication, with a few deep questions about the meaning of life thrown in for the sake of it.

As Dad has already given his view of how this all began, I should probably give mine too. To begin with, how I came up with the idea. One day, towards the end of 2008, I was walking back from school, and suddenly realised I was facing the prospect of several months of my life with nothing happening except school. This may not seem particularly unusual to many people, but the past two months had been full, and to me it seemed terrible. I started trying to think of something to do that would fill the time, and soon came up with the brilliant idea of a unicycle ride. A sponsored one. From John O'Groats to Land's End.

To try and see what people thought of the idea, I suggested that I would try unicycling from Coventry to Bristol in a day. I made no mention of the fact that this was a practice (probably very sensibly). My mum thought even this was very ambitious, and insisted that I would need lots of practice to cycle from Coventry to Bristol, that I should wait 'til the summer, that I needed a different diet in the run-up to this, and that someone would have to cycle with me. It was at this point that Dad walked into the room.

We had moved from Bristol to Coventry at the end of 2004. Joe, aged nine, was still in primary school, and had never even laid hands on a unicycle. Being uprooted from your home, your friends and all that you know, to move to a new place is not easy for a young, introverted, non-sporty lad. Joe had a few difficult years, finishing primary school and starting secondary school; he struggled with bullying at school, finding little way of expressing what he was going through other than through playing up at home. We can look back now, with a mixture of amusement and relief, at various incidents which highlighted the turmoil he was facing: our bedroom window, broken from the inside by a flying shoe; Joe's bunk-bed ladder sticking at right angles through his bedroom door; the garden hose directed at Helen (in the house) as she tried to mop up the overflow of all the bathroom taps turned on full. But we got through all that, and Joe, while still a fairly typical teenager in some respects (non-communicative; preferring to waste his time on inane computer games, rather than engaging in productive pursuits; and totally oblivious to all the housework he could be helping with), had nevertheless settled into life in Coventry. He had a great circle of friends, was doing well at school, and had found his own niche in his love of drama, circus skills and all kinds of performance.

Joe had started unicycling about five years previously, and it had become very firmly established as one of his foremost passions. Freestyle is Joseph's main type of unicycling. His Nimbus unicycle has a 20-inch wheel and a long frame. It is ideal for doing various tricks. Such a small wheel is not, however, any good for long distance riding. Joe also had a 26-inch Muni: a robust mountain

The unicyclist tries out his unicycle on the beach

unicycle. This is great for off-road unicycling, but although Joe had done a bit of this, he had not taken it up seriously.

There is something about a unicycle that inevitably seems to make people smile. On our many practice rides I enjoyed watching people, as we cycled past, catch a glimpse of Joe out of the corner of their eye, then turn in disbelief to watch him more carefully. I, in contrast, would be ignored – a middle-aged nobody on a bicycle – safe and sensible with my bicycle helmet and reflective yellow sash. We would also get lots of amusing (and some rather trite) comments from those we passed ('give us a wheelie then'). Small children would often point excitedly, desperate for their mothers to see this spectacle. It makes people happy, brightens their day. But I'd better let the expert tell you about unicycling:

I had started unicycling with the help of Steve at Shooting Stars Circus Skills. Unicycling, like juggling, is generally classified as one of many circus skills. However, it is mainly enjoyed by people who have no connection to any circus. There are several different forms of unicycling. Freestyle, which is my style, is about tricks. Generally, increasingly complicated variations on bunny hopping, idling, mounting, riding and wheel walking. Mountain unicycling, similar to mountain biking, involves riding down mountains. It is great fun. Trials unicycling involves riding courses, requiring bunny hopping great heights/distances onto very small/unstable platforms, riding up and down ramps and along very narrow poles/rails/planks. Arguably the most impressive unicycling skill, and great fun, but dangerous. Street unicycling, I'm not sure about. It seems to be similar to trials, and involves riding off drops and doing unispins/crankflips on the way down.

Road unicycling is what this book is about – riding long distances. But until that point I had not done any long-distance rides. Land's End to John O'Groats is not an easy cycle ride. Doing the route on one wheel adds an extra level of challenge – as well as having to constantly balance, there are no gears on the unicycle, and I can't freewheel on the downhill slopes either! Normal unicycling isn't hard, it just takes practice. Riding up hills on a 36-inch wheel is.

It was already decided that Dad would join me on a bicycle. He is a consultant paediatrician and does lots of research and training around sudden infant death. We decided between us that we would use the ride to raise money for a number of charities: FSID, a cot death charity which Dad is involved with; Servants, a group of Christian communities working in the slums of Asia, which Mum works with; and Spark in the Park, a fun, free activity week run by churches for children in Coventry, which my sister Esther and I help with. Later, with our practice ride out of the way, and our thoughts turning to the main ride, David our vicar decided to join us too. David was going to turn 60 and felt it would be a good way to celebrate. So there we had it – our team – the unicyclist, the vicar and the paediatrician.

But that's jumping ahead a bit. We were still in 2009, we'd only done one cycle ride of a mere 10 miles, and had a lot more training before even doing the 100 miles from Coventry to Bristol.

CHAPTER 3

MMX

The year of Our Lord two thousand and ten dawned bright and clear. And frosty. While a houseful of adolescents slept off the partying of the night before, I took Neo out for a walk. I decided on a slightly longer route than our normal circuit of the park. The iron-hard earth beneath my boots made a nice change from the usual squelchy mud down by Canley Ford. The white-frosted blades of grass glistened in the auroral light. Today would be an excellent day for a practice unicycle ride.

It was never to be. By the time I returned from my walk, the air of peace in our house had dissipated. Our two teenagers and the friends who had joined them for a sleepover were ensconced in the living room playing games on the Wii. It was to be a blobbing-out morning, and any training would have to go on hold.

As I walked, I thought back over our five years in Coventry. If 2010 got off to a contented start, the beginning of 2005 was very different. After a final, rather melancholy Christmas in Bristol, surrounded by packing cases, the removals people had arrived on the 30th, loaded everything into a van, and left Helen and me in an empty house – a kettle, a couple of mugs, vacuum cleaner and sleeping bags our only remaining comforts. The children slept over with friends and we collected them at seven in the morning, ready to get up to Coventry to meet the estate agents at nine to be let into the house ready for the removals van. The estate agents were not ready for us and had to phone round to find someone who could open up for us. The manager shouted at me when I expressed some frustration that we had just driven 100 miles and were stuck in a strange city with two tired and upset children, no friends to call in on, and no place that we could call home. When, three hours later, we finally got in, the house was in a state. The previous tenants had been a group of students. Not that I have anything against students – I'm all for learning. But they're not usually known for cleanliness and tidiness. I know that's a bit of a stereotypical generalisation, but by the time we'd scraped the layers of grease off all the kitchen surfaces, we were more than convinced that there might be more than a grain of truth to it.

So the eve of 2005 found the four of us (no dog then) sitting in a cold, dirty, rented house in a strange city, knowing no-one; tired and dejected, and once more surrounded by packing cases. Not the highest point in our family life.

I also set my thoughts on the year ahead. I'm not usually a fan of New Year's resolutions. They are too often vague, overambitious, of little worth, and rarely resolved. I am all for setting objectives, and in fact regularly have to do so in the course of my work. In training others in leadership skills, I promote objectives assiduously. But they must be worthwhile. Most resolutions however are either vague and unmeasurable, or wildly unachievable. 'I will be a better person this year' – in what way? How will you know whether you have been? 'I'm going to give up smoking' – again? Far better not to make them just for the sake of it, but rather to take some time out to really think through what you want to do, why you want to do it, how you will go about it, when by, who will hold you to account, and how you will know when you have achieved it. However, as they go, Joe's ambition of unicycling from Coventry to Bristol that summer wasn't a bad resolution – it was specific, measurable, achievable, relevant and time-bounded. And it would be a fun thing for the two of us to do.

Putting it into practice though was a different matter altogether. It had been three weeks since our first and only practice ride, so by the beginning of 2010, neither of us had managed more than 10 miles pedalling.

CHAPTER 4

A conversation

'Hi Joe, how was school?'
'Hm.'
'What did you do in school today?'
'Not much.'
'Uhuh, anything special?'
'Stuff.'
'M-hm. Supper's ready.'

Silence.

'Are you going to come down?'

More silence.

CHAPTER 5

The long, hard winter

January 16th. My last-minute suggestion that we cycle down to Warwick for Joseph's circus skills training almost paid off. Unfortunately I'd (a) left it rather late to suggest, and (b) underestimated the time it would take. I should have known better, it having been at least a month since our last (and first) practice ride, and judging by our average estimated speed then. We staggered up to Playbox Theatre 30 minutes after the start of the hour-long session. Joseph rather too tired to do much training at all.

England had finally broken out of the grips of arctic weather that had brought the country to a standstill. The prolonged freeze had closed schools, delayed bin collections, and left the roads, pavements and cycle tracks perilously slippery with ice and compacted snow. Even if we had wanted to do a practice ride, it would have been nearly impossible to do so.

For some reason Coventry seems to be in a snow shadow. Great swathes of snow clouds would sweep across the country from north, south, east or west. Whatever the direction, as they approached Coventry, they seemed to divaricate, dumping great drifts across the countryside, even as close as Solihull, but somehow missing us. Joe was devastated – each morning he would listen to the local radio, and hurry to check the council website for an update; each morning we would hear tales of thousands of schools closed; but the Coventry schools stubbornly stayed open, defying the wintry gods. No doubt there is a perfectly logical geographic explanation for this, but if you are a teenage lad, longing for an unscheduled holiday in which to throw snowballs at your friends and build a massive snowman, it is just not fair.

It came eventually: 1-2 inches, while the rest of the country seemed to have 8 or more; but enough to leave us too with treacherous roads and pavements. The schools closed, and the park swarmed with delighted youngsters and frosty snowmen.

For two weeks the frost hung on, until eventually the thaw came. The snowman in our garden was just a small mound, a mere shadow of its former self, and we, finally, could turn our thoughts once again to training.

February arrived. I like February. Although still clearly winter and unpleasantly cold, it is tense with expectation. The first snowdrops are adding little flecks of white to the overwhelming drab brown and green beneath our feet, while other bulbs push their viridian shoots up to the light, anticipating the day, soon, when they will add their yellows, mauves and whites to the show. Overhead, the long-quiescent trees are tingling with new life; ready to burst open at some pre-arranged signal. Even the birds seem to be catching on, convinced that spring can't be far away, and adding their calls to hasten its coming.

Joseph and I were finally getting going on some training – still rather ad-hoc, but we had both managed some reasonable cycle rides and the day before had again taken Neo for an extended run – this time it tied in well with collecting the car from the garage. It was to be his last time joining us – our cycling speed was picking up by now and it wouldn't be fair to expect Neo to go at our pace, or Joe to go at his. Off we went along the Kenilworth Road and up Gibbet Hill ('Why is it that everywhere I cycle seems to go up this hill?' was Joseph's comment). Down again to Crackley and along the disused railway to Burton Green. Then a slightly foreshortened final stretch to Cromwell Garage in Tile Hill where Jim had replaced an auxillary belt, tensioner and pulley, the wiper linkage assembly, two wiper blades and one wiper arm. Good for the car, not so good for the wallet. Overall we managed the 7½ miles in 65 minutes, so a definite improvement on last time. Then, with a bit of rearranging of seats, and a Twix to help us on the way, we got two guys, three wheels and a dog into our Ford Galaxy and returned home in time for some lunch.

CHAPTER 6

Hills

March came and went, and after a further cold spell, it felt as though spring had finally arrived. The daffodils were out in force, and buds were starting to appear on the magnolia and cherry trees. Joe, meanwhile, had bought himself a new unicycle with a massive 36-inch wheel. I'll let him pick up the story.

I realized some time ago that, if I was ever going to succeed in unicycling from Land's End to John O'Groats, I would need a better unicycle than the one I already possessed. Specifically, one with a larger wheel – fairly obviously, this means that the rider travels further with each rotation of the wheel, thus travelling faster with less effort. It has the same effect as changing gears on a bike. In theory.

Of course, this kind of unicycle is more expensive. Searching on unicycle.com, I found that the type I wanted cost somewhere in the region of £350. And, sadly, I don't get that kind of pocket money.

After I had planned various different ways of earning the money, a 36-inch unicycle appeared on eBay. Mum offered to get it for me as a birthday present, if I paid for part of it. The owner sold it for £250, so we made a three hour trip to collect it, along with some helpful advice about riding from Land's End to John O'Groats (the correct route from one end of Britain to the other being from south to north, rather than north to south). As the unicycle was meant to be a birthday present, I decided I would not ride it until my birthday – slightly under three months from the day I collected it.

I changed my mind about this as soon as I got home. (Probably a good idea, as waiting until my birthday would have left me less than a month to practise with it). I went for a ride in the park, and discovered that I could comfortably achieve a speed of 11 miles an hour. This was close to my fastest speed on the 26-inch muni, and was a speed that I could maintain for miles on the 36-inch, rather than a few hundred metres.

It was clear that buying this unicycle had been a good choice. I decided that, on this, I should be able to ride the 100 miles from Coventry to Bristol in 10 hours… possibly 12, allowing for stops.

A 36-inch wheel brings a whole new perspective

The warmer weather and the new unicycle gave a good excuse for a further practice ride – this time we managed 18.6 miles.

We set out late on Tuesday morning, once again heading off along the Kenilworth Road, this time without Neo. Joseph somehow managed to cut across Cannon Hill Road right in front of a funeral cortège – no respect for the dead there, nor for the fact that, had they been going faster, or he a bit closer, he could have been joining them on the wrong side. While I waited respectfully for it to pass, Joseph ploughed on 'til I finally caught up with him going up Gibbet Hill – even harder on the 36-inch wheel, as Joe himself explains:

In stating that I could easily sustain a speed of 10 to 11 miles an hour, I had overlooked one fairly major problem – the speed I had been doing in the park was on flat ground.

*For those of you who haven't had the experience of riding up a hill on a 36-inch unicycle, I will tell you this: It is hard. Well… perhaps that's not quite the right word. People assume that riding a unicycle is hard. It's not. Once you've learnt, the balancing becomes instinct, and it's easy. However, over long-distance rides, it does start to become hard, in a different way. An announcer at a unicycle race once stated that riding a unicycle was 60 times harder than riding a bicycle. I believe this is an exaggeration, but riding a unicycle **is** physically exhausting. It does tire you out more than riding a bike. And, after a while, the difference between unicycle and bike saddles starts to hurt. Even on the most comfortable gel saddles, it's not long before every bump causes you pain.*

But the worst problem is still riding up a hill. The person I bought the unicycle from said that on his 1,000- mile ride, he had enjoyed the bits with hills. Because they were interesting. He also said that he'd spent a large amount of time pushing the unicycle up them. Because riding up a hill on a 36-incher is like riding up one in the worst possible gear on a bike. And you can't change gears on a unicycle.

I endured the first four hills of the ride. It was halfway up the fifth one, a few hundred metres after Dad had confidently stated that we now had a flat section of the ride, that I got off and pushed for the first time. The hills had exhausted me.

A couple of hills later, I fell off. It was the first proper fall I'd had on a unicycle for over a year, and came as a bit of a shock. Nothing too serious though, just a couple of bleeding knees.

That wasn't his only fall though. After skirting round Kenilworth on Glasshouse Lane, we cut across to Cubbington, then a long stretch along the A445 past Bubbenhall and Martha – the methane gas converter at Ryton Pools. From Ryton we turned north, then back towards Coventry through Willenhall and Whitley Abbey and over the A444 Cheylesmore bypass. As we came down off the bridge to cross over Leaf Lane, Joseph managed to tumble forwards. Joseph himself was fine, but the small cycle computer that he got with the unicycle went flying out onto the road in front. Three cars appeared, as if from nowhere, the first two straddling the helpless gadget. Sadly the third went straight over it, blacking out the little screen and wiping out its impressive history of the 1,000 miles from Land's End to John O'Groats. Once more, Joseph had avoided the opportunity of joining a funeral party and I was glad it was just a replaceable bit of cycle equipment that went under the car tyre.

Cheylesmore is one of those strange Coventry place names whose pronunciation (Charles-more) bears little relation to its spelling. Foleshill (Fose-ull) is another, but perhaps the hardest is Stivichall, which has so confused people that it has had to take an alternative spelling of Styvechale on some road names. Cheylesmore actually has quite a history, with Cheylesmore Manor House dating from the 13th century and once the home of Edward the Black Prince. Far more importantly though, from Joseph's point of view, the Manor House had featured in an episode of *Dr Who* ('The Shakespeare Code'), as did the Ford Hospital almshouses just round the corner off Salt Lane. Sadly, most of Coventry's fine medieval buildings were demolished either before or after the war, to be replaced by rather a lot of ugly concrete; but a few stunning buildings and cobbled streets still exist if you care to look for them (although cobbled streets are not particularly good for unicycling on, especially on a 36-inch wheel). Not that we went past any of those fine parts of the city on this ride. We pressed on through Cheylesmore, and struggled up the final hill into Earlsdon and home:

The last hill of the ride was a long one. I pushed the unicycle all the way up; by that stage of the ride I had run out of energy. My legs were collapsing under me, and I barely had enough energy to ride on flat ground. I was going at less than half the speed of the beginning of the ride, and I was worried. The average speed of the ride was respectable, but if I was that tired after riding 20 miles, how could I manage 100? Or, for that matter, 50 a day for three weeks?

No doubt I would cope better with hills, and long distances, after more practice. No doubt I would find a mere 20-mile ride almost laughably easy by the summer. But just then I decided…

I hate hills.

CHAPTER 7

Five paces behind

A missionary to Afghanistan spent years, under the Taliban, campaigning for women's rights. She felt passionately about the inferior status of women in their culture, and lived among them, getting to know them, and urging them to speak out. Coming from a western culture of equality, she found it particularly irksome that the women would always walk five paces behind their husbands. Returning to the country years later, after the allies had 'liberated' the people from their oppressive overlords, she was distressed to see that the women still walked behind their husbands. Finding one of her old friends, she took her aside. 'Why,' she asked, 'after you have been set free, do you still live as though you are under such oppression? Why do you still walk five paces behind your husbands?' Her friend looked her in the eye. 'It's simple,' she replied, 'they reach the landmines first.'

On our travels, I tend to cycle five paces behind Joe. This has nothing to do with landmines, nor, for that matter, with parental liberation. Any apparent subservience is purely altruistic, so that I can keep an eye on him and ensure that overtaking traffic gives him a wide berth. The other reason, though it's a shame to admit it, is that he is 15 years old, fit and enthusiastic, and while I still pretend to a degree of fitness, I am nevertheless fully in my middle age and, at least on the uphill sections, even with the aid of gears, struggle to keep up.

Not so when going downhill. There, while Joe has to cautiously pedal his unicycle to prevent it running away from him, I can freewheel down, casting caution and care aside. That I did, to Joe's great annoyance on our next practice ride. These were now becoming a regular feature of our weekends, and gradually we were getting in shape for the rapidly approaching day of reckoning. On that occasion we set out eastwards to Draycote Water where Esther sails her Laser and earns pocket money teaching youngsters the joys of sailing. We started through the park and south through Finham, then got into a steady pace along past the Severn Trent sewage works, skirting through Stoneleigh and out to Ryton Pools. A sturdy bridleway took us through some woods then out to Princethorpe College, its magnificent edifice dominating that part of the Warwickshire countryside. It was after crossing the busy A423 that we came to the wonderfully quiet steep lane leading down from Frankton to the disused railway at Birdingbury. Less than a mile from Draycote, however, Joe rode over a nail and his tyre went flat. Helen was out, but fortunately Esther, having recently passed her driving test, loaded up the bike carrier and like a modern-day knight in shining armour, came to our rescue. How nice to have a ready-made chauffeur to hand!

Of course there are drawbacks to having your daughter able to drive. Like the pink furry dice. Esther decided (abetted by one of her teachers I might add), that by placing some pink furry dice in my car, I might be made too embarrassed to drive it, thus leaving it available for her personal use. I have heard of worse though, like the teenage lad who kept his used rugby kit and other unwashed clothes on the backseat of his mother's car. Esther's trick hadn't worked, but I was seeing less of my car, and over half-term when she was teaching sailing, I didn't get a look in all week. Still every cloud has a silver lining, and at least that forced me to cycle every day, building up my stamina.

We only managed 15 miles that day, but the following weekend did 28 coming back from a lunch with one of my work colleagues in Barnt Green. We stopped half-way for an ice-cold Pepsi at a pub, impressing the locals all sitting out for their beers in the early evening sun. On fine days like that, we were getting into a good stride and it was proving a great way to keep fit and explore the Warwickshire countryside.

From Joe's journal:

It is now almost the summer. May 25th, to be precise. A week till my birthday, and one month and one day till the ride. I am in the middle of my GCSE exams, with two already done, one tomorrow, and another five after that.

In terms of unicycling, things are going well. I have now done close to 200 miles of practice rides. Last weekend, I did a 30-mile ride, in very hot sun. It took three and a half hours (if I manage the same speed for the big ride, that will take around 11 hours 45 minutes). It was tiring, but I coped with the hills well, and I could still comfortably walk around by the end. Bristol is finally looking possible again.

Hills have virtually ceased to be an issue. I am used to them now, and though they are still tiring, I can cope well with them. I haven't had any more major falls, although I still have scars from the fall mentioned in the Hills chapter, and another big one from falling off while freemounting my 36-inch a month or so ago.

And, finally, I have started sorting out sponsorship. After going around school for a day with the sponsorship form, I am promised about £120. I still have several more people to ask. It's looking good… now I just have to do the ride.

CHAPTER 8

Jesus on a unicycle

Jesus never rode a unicycle (they weren't invented then). Nor to my knowledge did Gandhi, Martin Luther King, Mother Theresa or Nelson Mandela. They are all though in different ways, heroes. What makes a hero? Is it the performance of an act of bravery? Or a lifestyle of continued acts of bravery? Is it living a good life? And if so, by whose standards? And who defines who is a hero? I don't think my heroes will be the same as yours. Those I've listed above are well known, and probably many people would look on them as heroes, but not all. Nelson Mandela after all was a terrorist, so what qualifies him to be on the list? And what about those other, more personal heroes? People like Efren and Becky Roxas, who chose to live in a Manila slum when they could certainly have moved upwards and outwards, then after years in one run-down community relocated to another slum in Cambodia, continuing to serve the poor in that community? Or Jackie Pullinger, spending her life working alongside drug addicts in Hong Kong? Or my friend and colleague Sam Sophal?

Sam Sophal was a very ordinary Cambodian. He had grown up during the horrific Pol Pot era when many of his family were murdered during the genocide. He fled to the Thai border when the Vietnamese invaded his country, living for many years in a refugee camp. We met shortly after he returned to live in Cambodia, and he worked with me as a translator, motorbike driver and co-worker. He died prematurely of the tuberculosis contracted during those years as a refugee, for want of treatment that we would take for granted. It was only after he died that I realised just how much he had given of himself to support others in the community less fortunate than himself, going into debt and neglecting his own health in order to promote theirs.

Perhaps heroism, like beauty, is in the eye of the beholder. Does it rest in someone whose values and actions I admire or aspire to?

I admire Joseph's ability to ride a unicycle. But I certainly don't aspire to it. I have no wish to balance precariously on one wheel, constantly moving and throwing myself about just to stay upright. I am more than happy, thank you, with my feet firmly on terra firma, or at least with two wheels beneath me so I only need to worry about balance in one plane, not through a full 360 degrees. But I do admire it. I admire his ability to stick at it, his determination and persistence. If he decides to do something, he will generally do it, seeing it through to mastery. Of course, if he decides not to do something (at least if he decides not to do something I would like him to do), that determination suddenly ceases to be something I admire, and instead becomes a source of immense frustration and irritation. Nevertheless I do admire it; along with other qualities that set him apart – his incredible memory; his willingness to stand up for what he believes, even if that goes against the crowd; his lack of concern for what other people might think.

Joseph had first got into circus skills a couple of years previously when a friend introduced him to 'devil sticks' – two rubber-coated sticks with which he spun and tumbled a third. Circus skills training is not something you find on every street corner. We ended up travelling to Warwick, Stratford or Evesham most weekends to allow him to acquire progressively complex skills. Three-ball juggling; five-ball juggling; club juggling; two-person club juggling; fire-club juggling; tightrope walking; unicycling; giraffe unicycling; unicycling on a tightrope; blindfolded fire-club juggling whilst unicycling backwards across a tightrope. Well, maybe not the latter. Not yet at least.

I am usually a phlegmatic sort of character, not easily fazed. While others may have baulked at his first attempts at fire juggling, I was somehow OK with that. Even when he kept dropping them, sometimes perilously close to the can of kerosene used to fuel the sponges. Neo was fascinated, sitting at a respectful distance, watching those three enchanting flames dancing through the night, then sniffing haughtily and backing away whenever one of them crashed to the floor. Others may have worried about the safety of it all, but I was chilled. If you dropped them, you dropped them. We could always put the flames out if we needed to. What surprised me though was my reaction the first time Joe went on his kangaroo stilts. Finally he had achieved his ambition of being taller than me. Somehow it all seemed perilously unstable – just two small, flexible pegs to keep you upright and an awfully long way to fall if it all went wrong. I'm getting a bit more relaxed about that, but still anticipate something awful happening every time he tries to jump over something – what would happen if one of his stilts got caught on the way over? But as with so much else, he decided to master that, and so he has.

Juggling on a unicycle – an amazing feat of balance and coordination

I will add Joseph to my list of heroes. At least until the next time he ignores me when I ask him to help with the washing up.

It is said that it takes 10,000 hours to master anything. I suspect Joseph has a way to go on that, but he's certainly clocking them up. What about those other acts of heroism? When I think about it, all those whom I consider heroes have been persistent in living out what they believe. Most likely they've each put in far more than 10,000 hours of just being who they are, of living out their values. I think that's probably what I most admire – not the individual heroic acts, but a person with values I admire, who consistently lives them out.

CHAPTER 9

Another conversation

Being a true and complete transcript of a conversation held between Peter and Joseph during a 30-minute car journey to Stratford for circus skills training.

'Have a good time then, see you later'.

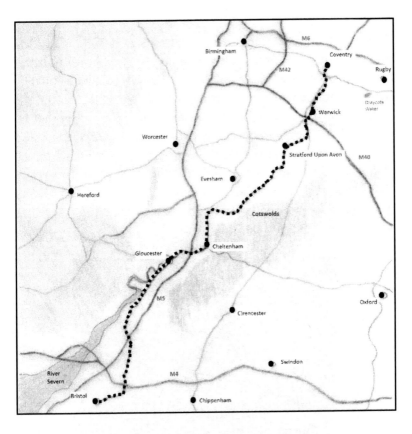

Map 2: The route from Coventry to Bristol

CHAPTER 10

June 27th

Coventry, being the home town of James Starley Esq., is an ideal place to start a 100-mile cycle ride. No, I too had never heard of him before we moved here, but he is, so I am reliably informed by the grand statue which we pass on our way out of the centre, the inventor of the bicycle. It may be more accurate to say that he modified and developed various two-wheeled contraptions into something more resembling the conveyance on which I travel, along with the Penny Farthings that are not that dissimilar to Joe's 36-inch unicycle. He was also the founder of the Coventry Sewing Machine Company, perhaps a far more legitimate claim, but less significant for our purposes.

June 27th – Joe and Peter set out from Coventry

After an early breakfast of cereal and bananas, we set off, as planned, at six o'clock, from outside Holy Trinity church. It was a beautiful, quiet morning as we pedalled past the statue of Lady Godiva, riding forth, 'clothed on with chastity', while all of Coventry, mocking their forebears' modesty, wander about her lovely form. All, that is, bar her erstwhile admirer, Peeping Tom. He, poor boy, is banished forever to Hereford Square, there to gaze not on her sensuous curves, but on the harsh concrete and brick walls of JJB Sports, and the monstrous glass appendage extending like an overgrown haemorrhoid from the base of the council offices. The front of those offices sport a magnificent clock from which Godiva herself rides forth each hour. She is another hero to add to my list. It may be no more than a legend, popularised by Tennyson's great poem, but if a great lady truly did sacrifice her modesty in opposition to her husband's unfair taxes, that is truly inspiring, and far more of a sacrifice than cycling a hundred miles to raise money for a children's holiday club.

We carried on out of the centre past Starley's memorial - a rather sad tribute to a great inventor. Fame, who stands atop, has lost both her arms (giving her a rather classic feel, but perhaps emphasising that, in spite of what the musical might say, she can't help us live forever); while Starley himself has lost his nose. Thence under the ring road (one of Coventry's least positive attributes, with tight entrances and exits forcing streams of traffic to criss-cross each other, vying for space). It is amazing that there aren't more accidents on it, but at least it does keep the centre relatively traffic-free and is well-endowed with subways and bridges for the likes of Joseph and me.

We went down through the Memorial Park, where Joseph and I had both done plenty of mini practice rides. The park itself was all set up for the Coventry Fun Run due to take place the following day, though of course, we wouldn't be able to take part this year (not that we ever have before, but it sounds good to imply that we are regularly active and community-minded). Then under the colourful and heavily graffitoed (apparently this habit originated in Pompeii, Rome and other ancient cities, at least so my Chambers dictionary tells me) subway beneath the A45 to Green

Lane. I quite like this subway, as you are greeted when you come up by a tremendous mural of the three *Italian Job* minis coming out of the wall towards you (apparently the sewer-tunnel scene was filmed in Coventry, a connection that was to prove pertinent as we continued on our ride). And so out towards Stoneleigh. This was taking a different route to our usual trip up Gibbet Hill and through Kenilworth, which we have done on so many of our south-bound practice rides. I'd always avoided Stoneleigh because of its horrendous hill. It had dawned on me, a week or so before the ride, that we probably climbed equal distances up Gibbet Hill itself and then through the centre of Kenilworth each time. Kenilworth may be a very pretty town, helped of course by its famous castle and picturesque Abbey Fields, but there does not seem to be any flat way through it. Looking again at the map, I realised that branching off right before Stoneleigh brought us along a very pleasant route through woods and hedged farmland, out past Ashow, Hill and Leek Wootton, and down the cycle lane into Warwick itself. Before we did so though, we passed the Severn Trent sewage works. Little did we know it at the time, but this was the first of many sewage treatment plants that were to grace us that day with their pervading odours.

Sewage aside, it was a beautiful, fragrant and cool morning, which we knew would not last, but which got us off to a fine start. We arrived in Warwick 20 minutes ahead of schedule. We found a nice little diversion through Priory Park into the centre of Warwick, stopping here for our first short break. I had scheduled in short breaks every 10 miles or so, with six more substantial breaks, dividing the route up into manageable sections. Pacing ourselves thus, I estimated the entire trip would take us 16½ hours, the total distance actually coming to 106 miles. As we passed the Playbox Theatre at Aylesford school (important, as this is one of Joseph's centres for circus skills training), the pungent smells of Severn Trent informed us that we were passing the third of our sewage works (we had passed a second, unknowingly, at Leek Wootton). Leaving Warwick we crossed the M40 on a useful cycle bridge, avoiding the busy Longbridge junction. This bridge leads into a secluded dead-end road where, to my consternation, we came across two white vans parked up, boxes of what I can only assume were stolen goods, laid out between them, and a number of shady-looking men wandering about. However, as they came more fully into view, I realised that they were accompanied by a police car with a number of officers questioning the miscreants and searching the vehicles. My guess is that the police had successfully busted a smuggling operation of some sort.

We took a little diversion through the pretty village of Barford with its lovely arched bridge over the river Avon. We were to stick close to this river Avon for most of the first third of our route, then finish up by the other Avon (I discovered that there are at least three in this country) in Bristol. This gave us a brief respite from the busy A429, which we soon came off again, to track across to Charlecote. The house at Charlecote was looking grand in the morning sun and its deer equally majestic, sticking their antlers up above the long grass. The B4086 through Tiddington into Stratford was rather busy, even at eight o'clock in the morning, and quite winding in places, with little room for cyclists to keep out of the way of passing cars.

Helen met us for a second breakfast (à la Merry and Pippin of *The Lord of the Rings*) at a little bistro by the river in Stratford. One of the great advantages to living in Coventry is having Stratford so close by. We've been able to come down and see several Shakespeare plays here, including the marvellous spectacle of David Tennant as Hamlet scooting in a psychotic frenzy round the Courtyard stage on a wheelie-chair. Joseph, along with his circus skills, is also doing a line in Shakespeare. One of his specialities is performing adulterated excerpts of *Romeo and Juliet*, somehow merging these with characters from *The Lord of the Rings* and *Star Wars* – to hear various scenes played out between Gollum and Darth Vader may lose something of the tragic beauty of that play, but invariably has everyone in stitches.

We set off from Stratford with Neo joining us for a lovely five-mile stretch along the Stratford Greenway. This disused railway has been converted into a cycle path and makes for comfortable, flat and traffic-free cycling. Joseph was on peak form now, charging ahead at about 12 miles per hour. I, meanwhile, ambled along at a more leisurely pace with Neo, pausing occasionally to allow him to sniff things on the way, and finishing off with a nice ditch for him to cool off in and quench his thirst shortly before the end of the Greenway at Long Marston. Here there was a very puzzling set of railway sidings and circuits marked on the OS map. Peering through the fence, it looked like an enormous scale model railway with narrow gauge tracks, but according to RailwayPeople.com, it is actually 15 miles of standage and five miles of running track that used to be one of the British Army's main strategic supply depots.

Helen left us at Long Marston, with Neo, who nevertheless seemed desperate for more, whining in the back of the car as they drove off to join us 11 hours later on the last stage of our endeavour. We carried on through the South Warwickshire and Worcestershire countryside. Our route took us on small winding roads down through Pebworth, Honeybourne, and Weston sub-Edge to our next stop at Broadway. We were however keeping up a good pace on this section and it seemed as though our regular training had paid off.

I have never really seen the appeal of Broadway, one of the Cotswold's most popular tourist attractions. I'm sure there is more that I haven't appreciated, but it seems to me to be little more than a very busy high street, teeming with tourists, and with lots of traffic passing through. We were pretty exhausted by the time we got there, so we just collapsed in the first bit of shade by the high street, rather than seeking out the village green.

The next stage of our route was perhaps one of the most picturesque, skirting round the edge of the Cotswolds, the escarpment rising up on our left. We were both very pleased to be travelling sub-Edge rather than sur-Edge. Heading southwest from Broadway, we came to the first steep hill up to Toddington. It was by now nearing midday and getting up to tropical temperatures. The heat was more in keeping with that which I had been used to in my years in Asia, though without the humidity, so nothing like as sticky. With a slight breeze it could have been quite pleasant, had we been lazing around, or freewheeling down-hill. We were doing neither. We got off and pushed the cycles up the hill to the roundabout by the northern end of the Gloucestershire and

Warwickshire railway. I was tempted to suggest that we catch one of their steam trains to cover the next stage down to Cheltenham, but that would have been cheating, and wouldn't have worked anyway. When we did stop at Cheltenham racecourse station for lunch, we found it was all closed for renovations as a landslide along the route had made the track impassable.

We pressed on along one of the hardest sections of our entire route. Although the scenery was lovely, the route from Broadway to Cheltenham was otherwise unremarkable, apart from yet another sewage works outside Buckland. From Toddington to Teddington, then down through Bishop's Cleeve, was all on busy roads with no cycle lane, and with cars, coaches and lorries all thundering past at horrible speeds. The sun was hot and there was little shade anywhere. We were getting through gallons of water and energy drinks, and still struggling to keep going. We thought it might prove better to divert off the A435 through Bishop's Cleeve, but in fact the town was very busy and I'm not sure this really helped. The final bit up the hill to the racecourse was another killer stretch that forced us to push the cycles up.

Exhausted, we sat down in the shade overlooking the station to eat our sandwiches, top up our sun cream, and drown ourselves in more water, by now getting rather warm (Helen had topped us up with frozen water bottles at Long Marston). We were joined by one of the railway engineers, who was able to tell us all about the history of the railway, what they were doing to restore it, how it was operating, and their plans eventually to take it through to Broadway and beyond.

Like Warwick and Stratford, Cheltenham was a good place to stop, having strong associations with Joseph's unicycling. This is where Joseph first got started on circus skills, at the Greenbelt Festival on Cheltenham Racecourse, just four years previously. It was also a good place to stop for lunch as we were by then half-way there. It was also a good place to stop for lunch as it was lunchtime. We were in fact a good half an hour ahead of schedule, but were not to maintain this advantage for long.

There are, of course, two ways of looking at your half-way point. On the one hand, we had already done half the route. On the other hand, we still had half the route to go. I personally prefer my glasses half-full, and the lunch break was a refreshing interlude. Joseph, perhaps naturally more of a glass half-empty sort of person, had the added disadvantage of having to work harder for this anyway. For him it was an essential breather, but hampered by the prospect of another nine hours' hard work ahead.

CHAPTER 11

On to Bristol

We've decided it would be a good idea to produce a range of car stickers saying 'I slow down for unicycles'. Most people are very polite, slowing down and giving us a wide berth, but there are certainly the exceptions: people who seem to take great delight in going as fast as they can with minimal clearance. Mostly these are young male drivers and the worst ones accompany that by beeping their horns at us. I'm never quite sure what their motivation is for beeping – whether it's done out of admiration, amazement, jealousy or just sheer testosterone-driven stupidity. It certainly seems to go hand in hand with those other adolescent males (of all ages) who shout out inane remarks such as 'lost a wheel have you?' or 'couldn't afford a proper bike?' or other totally unintelligible comments. In fact, we tend to get far more in the way of admiring and positive comments. The few people with whom we stopped to talk on the way were very impressed with what he was doing and that was always an encouragement.

Our friendly railway engineer pointed us on our way from Cheltenham Racecourse, suggesting an alternative route through Pittville Park by the duck ponds. This was very pleasant, but rather ruined by having to then wind our way through a housing estate, taking a couple of wrong turns down dead-end streets on the way.

We stopped at a pub in the centre of Gloucester for two pints of Pepsi, ice-cold and very well earned. The barman, John, was being ribbed mercilessly by the locals for working up a sweat just by pulling a pint. I must say, I shared some of their disdain, having by then travelled 65 miles in the hot sunshine outside. The bar itself could not have been more than three yards from end to end, and it was nice and cool inside. Nevertheless, John was friendly and good-natured about the teasing, and as well as pouring the Pepsi, refilled our water bottles with ice and water to see us on our way. Joseph, keeping up the 'glass-half-empty' approach, pointed out that we had by now gone further than we had on any of our practice rides and we still had 45 miles to go.

Two more sewage plants as we headed out of first Cheltenham and then Gloucester, brought our total up to seven. A Defra report on sewage treatment in the UK told me that every day more than 11 billion litres of waste water are treated in the UK's 9,000 sewage treatment works, so although it seems a lot to us, we have only scratched the surface of experiencing the country's sewage. I am full of admiration for those people who work in these plants day in day out, to keep our country clean and fresh. I dread to think where we would be without them. So I will add them to my list of heroes, along with those who collect our rubbish, sweep our streets, clean our public buildings and do countless other thankless jobs.

The route from Gloucester to Berkeley was a really lovely stretch of cycling, although it was in the hottest part of the day which took the edge off it a bit. This section, following National Cycle Route 41, was relatively flat along the Severn Estuary, partly along the towpath of the Gloucester and Sharpness Canal, an impressive navigable ship canal, with its grand swing bridges. The bridge keepers were very friendly, and several people along the canal were interested and impressed with what we were doing and how far we had come. In other places it flitted backwards and forwards between the canal and the river. I told Joseph that Helen and I had once been through all those villages chasing the Severn Bore, and he conjured up a delightful image of the two of us going from village to village enquiring after a tedious old gentleman who would then regale us with interminable tales of the river. The reality is very different, and the Severn Bore is quite an incredible natural phenomenon. I remember waiting on the banks of the Severn, its mudflats exposed by the low tide; in the distance you hear a roar that gradually increases as it approaches, seeming to gain momentum as a great tidal wave then comes towards you, and the whole landscape is transformed in a matter of seconds as the river rises several feet. If you are quick enough, you can then jump in your car and scoot up-river a bit further to catch it at the next point.

There are some lovely-looking pubs along the Severn Estuary, but, nice as it would have been to linger, we pressed on until we got to the Salutation Inn just beyond Berkeley. Berkeley itself is a very quiet town given its crucial global importance as the place where Edward Jenner discovered vaccination. It is quite amazing to think how many lives have been saved because of that; although his experimentation on James Phipps, the son of his gardener, was totally unethical by today's standards.

From Berkeley we set off for the hard slog out of the Severn valley, pushing our cycles up the steep hill to Tortworth. From there it was easy riding down past Leyhill prison to Cromhall, where we stopped at the Royal Oak for supper. Only we didn't as, when we got there, we found that the Royal Oak was vacant and to let. Nevertheless, Helen met us there with bananas, Lucozade and Ibuprofen to keep us going. After unsuccessfully trying to help someone get his go-cart started, we carried on to the Rose and Crown at Rangeworthy, where Helen was once again waiting for us, this time with the added bonus of a delicious prawn, ham and pepperoni pizza.

The proprietors and clientele of the Rose and Crown were full of hospitality and they gathered outside to see us off on the last leg of our journey. A marked cycle path between Cromhall and Rangeworthy then gave way to wiggly lanes through Iron Acton and Frampton Cotterell. A short distance further, at Coxgrove hill, we joined the Dramway and thence the Bristol-Bath cycle path. The ruins of the old Mangotsfield station, the colourful pencil wigwams and the bramble bushes flanking the cycle path below Rodway Hill were all familiar territory, and it felt strangely like coming home again. It was here that Joseph, years ago, did his first ever (bi)cycle ride of any substance, with a day trip along this cycle path to Bath and back. A fraction of the distance we had covered this day, but for a five(ish) year old as he was then, a major achievement.

Esther and her friend Amy met us at Station Road to cheer us along, and Neo joined us again for the last few miles into Bristol itself. Now, in the cool of the evening, he was thoroughly invigorated, and set the pace, even finding the energy to go chasing ahead after a fox until it scampered into some impenetrable bushes. With the drink and pizza taking effect, the heat dissipating, and the prospect of the end of our journey getting steadily closer, Joseph and I too were reinvigorated, and cycled down this home stretch at a cracking pace. Through the Staple Hill tunnel, then down through Fishponds, past a random upside-down fish, Clay Bottom, Rose Green and Easton; and so to Lawrence Hill and the end of the cycle path, and into the centre of Bristol. Apart from being our home for most of the first half of Joseph's life, Bristol, like Coventry, was an excellent place to end our cycle trek. In 2008, Bristol was named the UK's first cycling city, with bicycle rental schemes, dedicated cycleways and a host of other initiatives to encourage commuters and others to get out of their cars and onto their bikes (though not perhaps their unicycles). It is also home to Sustrans whom we have to thank for many of the cycle routes on which we have travelled.

Negotiating the redeveloped Temple Meads area, we carried on past St Mary Redcliffe Church, the Welsh Back and so across Queen Square to end our epic journey by the fountains on Broad Quay. As we cycled up, a Canadian busker gave us a celebratory drum roll on an African drum, and Esther, Amy and Helen all cheered as Joseph cycled in triumph through the finish tape. We had done it.

CHAPTER 12

Looking back: Coventry to Bristol

Joe's account of this first mammoth ride:

I had ridden one hundred and six miles in a day. From Coventry to Bristol.

I can't say I enjoyed most of the ride at the time – a lot of it was just repetitive pedalling along roads. I was in slight pain a lot of the time. Coming up to Cheltenham Racecourse just before lunch was probably the worst bit – I was exhausted, feeling quite sick, and my legs were aching. Most of the middle of the day was far too hot – it was marginally better than riding through a rainstorm, but still very tiring. For much of the section before supper, I was riding very slowly – probably just over 10 miles an hour, but only just. (Most of the times I looked at the speedometer, my riding speed was about 13 mph, going up to 15 mph occasionally. With the sections stopping at traffic lights, and getting off to cross roads, and the slow section in the middle, the average speed was 11.3 mph). There were times when I was fairly near to collapsing through lack of energy. And I don't know what was going through my head during the ride – I think I may have gone mad a couple of times, and was reduced to counting the seconds for about half an hour somewhere in the middle. I doubt that I will ride that far in one day again for a very long time.

In terms of the good parts… Dad stated in the opening chapter that this might be an opportunity for some Father-Son bonding. I don't know how well that worked, but I don't think there are many parents who have accompanied their children on 100-mile unicycle rides. And we did have a few good laughs during the ride.

I did enjoy two sections of the ride. The few miles along the Stratford Greenway were very nice – it was flat, there were other cyclists, Neo was running with us, it wasn't too hot, and I was riding at 14-15 mph most of the time. The other very nice bit was riding along the cycle path into Bristol. From nowhere in particular, I had suddenly found large amounts of energy again. I was reaching very good speeds again for the first time in several hours. The sun had gone down, so it was nice and cool, and I suddenly found myself recognizing parts of the cycle path, from the bike rides we used to take down it. Also, I had nearly finished by that point, which was nice.

The pizza that I had for supper was very nice.

Also, there were several moments of humour. In the first half of the ride, we rode past six sewage works. Although a couple of these smelt a bit bad, it did become quite amusing after the first couple of times. There was the usual reaction from passers-by/people at the stops, which still amuses me occasionally. Finally, there were several ridiculous road signs – there was a sign advertising 'Porky's Good Food – We sell coal'. There was one row of signs telling us to 'Remember!' There were a couple of others which I've forgotten. And, finally, there was one section of cycle lane that was marked with about 80 pictures of bikes spread out over a few hundred metres!

So, overall, it wasn't too bad. And the problems were definitely worth it. As I said, I'm not desperate to try that long a distance again. Or, at least not in one day… I could probably manage 60 or 70 a day, going from Land's End to John O'Groats…

CHAPTER 13

Unconditional Cycling

Dr Ross Campbell, along with many other parenting gurus, tells me that what Joseph needs from me is unconditional love (*How to Really Love Your Teenager*, Authentic Classics, 2006). He does not give any advice however on accompanying your son on a long-distance unicycle ride. At least as far as I'm aware he doesn't. I can't be absolutely sure as I rather gave up on the book part-way through. Not that it isn't good; it's just that I have a bit of an issue with books on parenting. That's one of the reasons why I have never written one. As a paediatrician I find a lot of parents ask me for advice on how to bring up their children. I'm always very hesitant to offer such advice. After all, I can hardly claim to be a perfect parent, even if such an entity were to exist. And if I were, I probably wouldn't be the best person to offer advice to anyone else. And anyway, what right have I to assume that what works for me and my family would necessarily work for anyone else? No, I think I shall stick to a bit of empathy, positive affirmation and glimmers of hope.

Some sociologists refer to it as 'unconditional positive regard', a horrible phrase which I think encapsulates a lot of what is wrong with sociology (there's a lot that's right with it too). Love is so much more than positive regard, whether it is unconditional or not. What about the affection, nurture, fun, hope, frustration, pain and that myriad of other emotions, attitudes and actions that go with love? I don't think love is always positive in its regard. I am hardly going to be unconditionally positive about my toddler when they are throwing the most almighty tantrum in the middle of a supermarket with everyone else looking on, or at my teenager when he shouts at his mother and slams the door in her face. But that doesn't stop me loving him.

I sometimes think that teenagers have a great capacity for showing their parents unconditional negative regard.

But that is perhaps a very biased view of adolescence, and maybe what appears to me as 'UNR' is really nothing of the sort when viewed from Joseph's perspective. I think we will both have to accept that we each experience both positive and negative feelings towards the other, and that none of it is entirely unconditional. We may not have a perfect father-son relationship, but I reckon it's not too bad.

It was a balmy evening in July. Helen and Esther were both out. Joseph and I ate our supper together in silence. I then did the washing up, while Joseph sat at the computer in the other room, interspersing homework with computer games and Facebook. His unicycle was hanging up in the garage where we put it two weeks previously, after our marathon ride. It was an unconditional ride, as was all the training beforehand. Perhaps it hadn't transformed our communication and family relationships, but I was glad we did it and I was game for the 1,000 miles from Land's End to John O'Groats.

PART 2
Land's End to John O'Groats

CHAPTER 14

All in a good cause (or three)

Joe's ride from Coventry to Bristol had inspired many of our friends, family, colleagues and fellow church members, as a result of which Joe raised over £600 for Spark in the Park. 'Spark' proved to be a mad week of fun and games, with a few thousand Coventry youngsters throwing themselves into the action in the Memorial Park. Joseph, Esther and a host of other volunteers from Coventry churches spent long hours each day balloon-modelling, face-painting, and subjecting themselves to the 'gunge shower' (and yes, it was what the packet said…) And so we moved into the autumn, and the return to school, darkening evenings and the looming spectre of A-levels and GCSEs. I had expected that life would get a little calmer, at least for a few months. Joe had other ideas:

After successful auditions for the Advanced Circus group and the Young Shakespeare Company at Playbox Theatre, I have another couple of activities to keep me busy. I'm still really enjoying our church youth group, and also looking after the younger kids after church (when they play exciting games such as 'Walkaround', which involves… walking around). In terms of upcoming events: I'm looking forward to exam leave, when I should be able to get large amounts of unicycling practice amongst the revision.

Over the dark, cold winter months, while Joe threw himself into every activity bar revision, I took the time to start planning our journey from Land's End to John O'Groats. With the aid of the Cyclists' Touring Club, Sustrans, a large terrain map of Britain and the ever-helpful 'g-maps pedometer' website, I managed to plot out a route. My primary goal was to avoid hills as much as possible. For most of England (from Taunton to Berwick) this wasn't too difficult, although it did necessitate traipsing over to the east of the country, a much longer route than the usual west-of-Pennines one. This added a good two to three hundred miles to the total distance, but to my mind it seemed worth it for a flatter ride. Unfortunately, try as I might, there seemed to be no way of avoiding the hills at either end. Cornwall and Devon seemed to consist of nothing but tiny roads going up and down very steep hills; while the centre of Scotland was dominated by the brown mass of the Cairngorms. Either way, we would have to just do it.

As well as planning the route and the various logistics needed to support this ride, we started to turn our mind to our plans for fundraising. We decided it would be good to support three charities, each of which we had direct links with: we wanted to support next year's Spark in the Park, hopefully with an even bigger sum; the Foundation for the Study of Infant Deaths (FSID), a national charity of which I was on the Board of Trustees; and Servants, an international charity for which Helen worked as the UK coordinator and international administrator.

We first got to know about Servants in 1993. I was coming to the end of paediatric registrar training, and it seemed like a suitable time to consider a career break. Helen and I had always wanted to spend some time working overseas in a developing country, so we set about looking for opportunities. Having been brought up in Hong Kong, I was particularly drawn to Southeast Asia, and initially had my sights set on Thailand. I had spent a wonderful few months at a Leprosy Mission hospital in Chiang Mai as a medical student, and had fallen in love with the country – the beauty and friendliness of its people, and their easy-going approach to life, summed up in that ubiquitous Thai phrase, 'Mai Pen Rai': 'it's OK', or 'never mind'. We later found that the Cambodians had two similar phrases: 'Ot ai te' and 'Ot pannee ha te', both conveying the same sense that nothing really matters. To me these phrases reflect some of the fatalistic, cyclical thinking in Buddhist philosophy, and we found the attitude both inspiring and frustrating. On the one hand, it meant that those we met and worked with rarely got cross or reacted when things went wrong; on the other hand, it did mean that problems, failings and injustice could carry on unchecked, lying hidden beneath the surface.

While I was dreaming of Thailand, Helen, being far more socially aware, pointed out that it didn't really count as a developing country and that its neighbour Cambodia was far more needful of international support. At the time Cambodia was just coming out of years of civil war and disruption under the Pol Pot regime of the 70s, and the ensuing Vietnamese occupation. With a UN peacekeeping force in place, tens of thousands of Cambodian refugees were returning from border camps in Thailand, and starting to resettle in Phnom Penh and elsewhere. Poverty was rife, and the rapid urban expansion, coupled with a total lack of any infrastructure, meant that there were huge needs among the population.

We started exploring opportunities for going to Cambodia, but none were forthcoming. And then, out of the blue, in May 1993, a friend contacted us to tell us that he knew of an organisation in Cambodia who were looking for a paediatrician for a one-year post on a new health team. It sounded ideal, and within a month I was out in Phnom Penh. Hence began an 18-year relationship with Servants.

My paediatric friends and colleagues were all extremely positive and encouraging of this venture. All, that is, except one eminent professor of paediatrics who advised me not to go to Cambodia, commenting that if I did take a year out to go overseas, I could effectively say goodbye to an academic career! Not so David Baum, Professor of Child Health in Bristol, who went on to become president of the Royal College of Paediatrics and Child Health, before he tragically died while on a sponsored cycle ride in 1999. David was incredibly enthusiastic and encouraging of my involvement with Servants. He was an inspiration, demonstrating that it was possible to pursue an academic career while remaining passionate about working for those who were most vulnerable.

Servants to Asia's Urban Poor (to give it its full name) came into being in the early 1980s when a pioneering New Zealander, Viv Grigg, set off with six fellow Kiwis to go and live in a slum in Metro Manila. Viv, who had been working as a missionary in the

Philippines, had been appalled by the poverty he saw there, and troubled by the apparent blindness of the church to issues of oppression and social justice. He concluded that the only way to make a real difference in the lives of people living in slum communities was to get alongside them – not to come in as powerful westerners with all the answers, to do things for the people – but to go and live with them, to learn from them, and to empower them to do things for themselves. His inspiration came from the 'incarnational' model of Jesus' own ministry, and was neatly summed up in an ancient Chinese poem which he quotes in his book, *Companion to the Poor*:

Go to the people,
Live among them.
Learn from them.
Start with what they know.
Build on what they have:
But of the best of leaders,
When their task is accomplished,
Their work is done,
The people all remark
'We have done it ourselves.'

Servants describes itself as 'an international network of Christian communities living and working in the slums of Asia and the West, participating with the poor to bring hope and justice through Jesus Christ'. We were immediately attracted to the committed, passionate people on our team in Cambodia. Our fellow team members had left the security of their homes, families and jobs to come and live in slum communities in Phnom Penh, living alongside the poor, and working with them to see transformation in their communities. The team in Phnom Penh was focused around a community health programme, and during our year there we saw the development of community based nutrition and outreach clinics, immunisation programmes, a project for disabled children, health education and much more. It was an inspiring but challenging year and we were sad to leave at the end.

After returning to the UK, Helen remained involved with Servants, taking on coordination of the UK home base and, over time, getting more and more involved in international administration and leadership. This brought with it the exciting opportunity of remaining in touch with all that was going on, not just in Phnom Penh, but with other teams in the Philippines, India and other Asian countries. This was demanding work, and alongside the amazing stories of transformed lives and communities, there were tales of struggles and heartaches; of projects that had failed, and people who had let them down. But the faithfulness of these individuals continued to inspire us, and was a strong driving force behind our fund-raising through the trip.

While Helen's role in Servants continued to grow over the years following our return from Cambodia, my career took a different direction, much more firmly based in this country. I completed my paediatric training and we moved with our young family to Bristol where I took on a part-time consultant post, as a job-share with one of my previous colleagues. I loved working with Maria – sharing the role meant we could bounce ideas off each other, and we worked well together; and the part-time nature of the work meant I could spend some time with my family and develop other interests, including a growing involvement in child protection work, starting a PhD, and eventually helping develop services for responding to sudden infant deaths.

In the late 1990s, there were about 10-15 sudden infant deaths each year in the Bristol area. This was about a quarter of the numbers just a decade earlier, reflecting a similar national reduction in the rates of sudden infant death syndrome (SIDS). This reduction in SIDS was one of the major public health success stories of the late 20th century. Research in the 1970s and 80s had identified major risk factors for SIDS, particularly the dangers of sleeping babies on their tummies. A national campaign, spearheaded by FSID, encouraged measures to reduce the risks, including placing babies 'Back to Sleep'. SIDS rates fell across the country and probably thousands of infant deaths have been avoided as a result. FSID continued to campaign on behalf of families, to fund research into SIDS and to support bereaved parents. With the fall in SIDS rates, the profile of affected families also changed, with SIDS predominantly affecting some of the most vulnerable in our society: young single mothers, those living in poverty or in deprived communities, smokers and those with drug or alcohol problems. Further research identified a range of different causes that could lead to sudden unexpected death in infancy, but the majority remained unexplained, a situation that added to the grief these families experienced.

While most of these sudden infant deaths were clearly from natural causes, it was equally clear that a small proportion were likely to be a consequence of inappropriate parenting and neglect, or even of more deliberate, covert homicides. The problem, of course, was that it was rarely possible to distinguish these rare maltreatment-related deaths from the vast majority of natural SIDS. When a baby died unexpectedly, the police needed to carry out their investigations to exclude homicide, again often adding to the distress of bereaved families. It was in that context that I first got involved in responding to unexpected deaths. With my background in interagency child protection, I was able to work with colleagues in both the police and health services as they strove to develop sensitive ways of investigating these deaths while supporting these families through such a difficult time. I had the privilege of working alongside Professor Peter Fleming, a leading international SIDS researcher, and the even greater privilege of meeting with and learning from families whose infants had died suddenly and unexpectedly.

We set ourselves the rather ambitious target of raising £6,000 to be divided between the three charities – 10 times the amount we had raised the previous summer. It seemed a far-off target, but we launched into it with great gusto, setting up an online giving page and starting to publicise it at every opportunity. I was totally impressed by people's generosity in response. We received lots of encouraging emails – some not so complimentary to me though: 'I am sure your son will cope admirably on his unicycle, however 1,000 miles on a bicycle for you makes me a little worried!!' Still, in the space of just a couple of weeks we managed to raise our first £1,500, so were well on our way to our target, and it was clear that we couldn't duck out of the challenge.

CHAPTER 15

Back into training

Bank Holiday Monday. I woke up to the sound of dripping outside our bedroom. The gutter had become blocked, and the rain sweeping across the country seemed to be dropping mostly on our roof. It hadn't rained for two months. Our garden was wilting. Farmers were reporting ruined crops. So a day of solid rain was a blessing. Just not on the day we had chosen to do a 120-mile overnight practice ride to Weedon and back to visit my parents. The BBC weather pages looked grim, a thick band of rain making its way from west to east. We decided to delay our start on the basis that the worst of it may have blown over by lunchtime. We were to have no such luck. The BBC review of the weather for the 30th May stated that, 'Outbreaks of rain developed through southwest England, Wales, the Midlands and northern England by dawn, becoming steadily more persistent and heavy in places during the early morning. Eight to 15 mm fell quite widely through this zone. The rain became less heavy and more intermittent by the end of the morning as it moved eastwards into the east Midlands and parts of East Anglia and southeast England.' We, however, did not reap the benefits of that eastward progression, as it simply meant that the heavy rain followed us all the way, finally clearing up shortly after we reached our destination.

Our waterproofs worked though, and we all stayed dry above the waist. All three of us had opted for shorts, so the legs didn't matter. Joe's shoes were soaked through in no time; my new waterproof walking shoes did much better, but even they, by the end of the day, were drenched. David, our third team member, had opted for sandals.

The three cyclists setting off in the rain

The ride itself was great, in spite of the rain, and we made it all in one piece, Joe and I still fit for the return ride the following day. We didn't notice it at the time, but the wind had been behind us the whole way, which I'm sure helped, both in terms of speed and with the impact of the rain. The following day was a lot harder – the morning seemed to be all uphill and against the unremitting wind, which made the hills seem twice as steep. Still it didn't rain, so that made up for it.

We actually coped pretty well with the hills on the first day. We only ended up walking up two – a long 11% gradient up Deddington Hill to Warmington, which defeated us all, and later in the day an equally steep climb to Padbury. At the top of Deddington Hill we spotted the National Herb Centre with an inviting café. I had a moment of doubt as we cycled up the lane that they may only serve strange-tasting herbal infusions, but we were in luck with some excellent curried chickpea soup, coffee, and hot chocolate – all totally delicious, warming and refreshing. So much so that Joe and I stopped there again for lunch the next day. The staff had put up one of our flyers and one generous lady, who had passed us earlier in the day, gave us some sponsorship money.

The day after this ride was Joe's birthday. Sixteen years. We celebrated it in style by arranging several photoshoots and interviews. FSID had sent out a press release, and all three local Coventry papers picked up on it, so sent their reporters and cameramen to get more details, and lots of posed photos. Joe's knee was aching and seemed set to scupper the whole project, as each time he tried to mount his unicycle for another photo he was in agony. After presents and cake spread through the day, we all trooped down to Priory Place for a live interview on BBC Coventry and Warwickshire. David met us down there, on his bike, none the worse for wear, though he did admit he was glad he hadn't had to do a second day.

After a few days' rest, and with the aid of some support bandages, Joe's knees seemed to have recovered, and he was back to doing regular practice rides. At least until one fateful day when he managed to break his seatpost.

Joe's Blog:

I was riding to Warwick for circus training – the fourth ride in four days, having covered 80 miles over the previous three days, and my seatpost snapped. A good clean break, just where it joins the saddle. Luckily, the saddle was still just about attached, so I managed to ride the final mile. It's not an experience I would recommend, though – riding through the centre of Warwick with a broken unicycle is kind of scary...

Still, Roger at Unicycle.com managed to put a new one in the post, and Joe was once again back on the road.

We were by then well into the summer, and, in spite of exams, the unicycle seemed to be dominating our lives. It felt as though every spare moment was spent either preparing for the trip, raising sponsorship money, or going out on practice rides. From Joe's perspective, the training was going well, as he noted at the time:

I'm on exam leave at the moment, giving me plenty of time for training, and practising freestyle. (No, I shouldn't be revising – I've only got two exams left.) It's beginning to seem as if half the population of Coventry has seen me on one of my unicycles, and though this may be a slight exaggeration, the word is certainly getting around about the ride. Several people have seen me in the paper, several people have sponsored me, and several people have made encouraging comments as they pass me in the park.

So with all these people expecting me to complete the ride, I need to make sure that I can actually do it. Training is going well, though. Walking the dog this morning, I noticed my speedometer telling me that I've now done over 1,000 km of practice rides. 1,002.8, to be precise – 623.1 miles. Realistically, I've probably done closer to 700, as I've done a few longish rides without the speedometer, and I did 50 miles or so on my old one, before it was run over.

Whichever way you look at it, it's a fairly impressive distance. The worrying thing is that it's only just over half the distance I'll be covering on the ride...

David joined us when he could, and he and I even managed one ride on our own, unconstrained by Joe who, with the confidence of youth, had decided he had done enough practice rides and had arranged for his youth group to come round and bake cakes for a cake sale in aid of Spark in the Park. After a hard climb east out of Coventry to Corley Moor, David and I were able to freewheel at uninhibited speeds down the gentle declines to Meriden. Then up a steeper hill the other side and so back to Coventry to find our kitchen swarming with teenagers, flour, butter, icing sugar and other delicacies.

The teenagers managed to raise a fair bit of money for Spark in the Park, and by now our own sponsorship was starting to come in thick and fast. We were well on our way to reaching our £6,000 target.

That summer seemed to be the season for sponsored challenges. Friends of ours ended up doing the Coventry Fun Run, the Run for Life, the Three Peaks Challenge, the Kilworth Challenge, the Isle of Wight cycle ride, and a bungee jump in New Zealand. The maddest was a team from the Nexus Trust music college who did a 72-hour football game for their rag week. Joe and I cycled out to Hinkley one Saturday to watch them for a bit. They had only been going 10 hours by then and it seemed reasonably sedate. They did make it in the end, but were pretty well on their last legs by the end of the 72 hours. Almost as mad, to my mind, was the group of unicyclists who set out to do the London to Brighton cycle ride. At least, I would have considered that mad were it not for the fact that my own son was one of them, that I was accompanying him (on a bicycle), and that this was, for us, just a warm-up.

Most people consider cycling from London to Brighton as a major challenge, an end in itself, and a great opportunity to raise money for charity. Two years ago I probably wouldn't even have contemplated doing it, seeing it as an unnecessarily painful way to raise money and a form of torture that I could quite happily live without. But my sense of normality had changed, so off we set.

Joe's Blog:

So at 7:15 on Saturday morning, we found ourselves at Clapham Common with a group of unicyclists, getting ready to ride to Brighton. Here's how it happened: One of the group had asked to take part in the British Heart Foundation London to Brighton ride, which took place a few weeks before. He was instantly refused on health and safety grounds, for reasons beyond our understanding. Posting a thread about it on the unicycle forum, he soon got together a group of around 15 unicyclists to ride it with him on this particular Saturday. Seeing a good opportunity for training, I got in on the act.

Of course, things didn't work out quite as planned. Several drop-outs meant that only nine unicyclists, including myself, started the ride. Among them were Lejog record holders Roger Davies and Sam Wakeling, with their geared unicycles. Accompanying us were three cyclists, including my dad, and three support vehicles.

And so we set off, half an hour later than planned. The first 20 miles took us over four and a half hours, due to slow riding and long breaks. Dad and I were at the front of the group, meaning we had to wait about an hour at each rest stop for the stragglers to get there and have a break.

This was far too relaxed to give Dad and me any decent practice, so on the third leg, I tried tailing Roger, who was leading the way on his geared unicycle. Incredibly, I actually managed it, leaving Dad behind after the first five miles. Towards the end of the leg, when Roger put his unicycle in gear, I couldn't keep up, though I caught up again going up Turner's Hill. By this point, three riders had dropped out. Among them, incredibly, was Sam, after his geared hub had broken.

After Turner's Hill, Alan, who had led the way for the first two legs, got bored. He left the stop 20 minutes before everyone else, and we didn't see him much until the final stretch. Twenty miles later, we reached Ditchling Beacon – a very big hill, less than 10 miles outside Brighton. At this point, Sam rejoined the ride on someone else's unicycle, and he and Roger sailed up the Beacon without much trouble. Liam managed the hill with a stop in the middle. Alan, Ben and Geoff walked up most of it. Dad rode it all, though very slowly. I had stopped at the bottom to wait for the camera crew to give me a helmet cam – they wanted to film the hill. This gave me the pleasure of overtaking four unicyclists, and Dad, as I struggled my way up the hill. Strong winds as I reached the top blew me off just before the very peak, but I was only a couple of metres away. Close enough.

From there, it was downhill all the way into Brighton. I overtook Alan for the third time in the ride, and was one of four unicyclists who crossed the finish together, a fair way ahead of the others (unsurprisingly, Sam and Roger were there, and Ben, who caught us up going down the hills). As a group, we had taken nearly 12 hours to ride 56 miles. Conclusion: not the fastest training ride ever, but still good fun.

Compared to the impending doom of Land's End to John O'Groats, London to Brighton seemed a mere lazy jaunt. But comparisons are dangerous things. The three weeks we were planning to take doing the End-to-End trip paled into insignificance beside Joe's unicycling friends, Roger and Sam, who the previous year had done it in just six days. Still, for me it was an achievement, particularly managing to cycle up the notorious Ditchling Beacon. Even more, I marvelled at the stamina of both Joe and the other unicyclists who did the route. However, we couldn't rest on our laurels, particularly after having taken so long to complete the distance, so we followed it up the next day with another, more energetic training ride.

Joe:

After the slow ride on Saturday, Dad and I really needed to do a decent training run. So, driving back up towards Coventry, Mum dropped us off near Oxford, ready to ride the 50 miles back home.

Shortly after setting off, I realised I had far too much energy, undoubtedly due to the large amounts of cheesecake I had eaten that morning. So, bored of pacing myself, and inspired by the exploits of Roger and Sam, I pushed the speed up a bit. At some point near the beginning Dad needed to stop, but assured me he would catch up. He did so, but it took him most of the rest of the leg. (Apparently, it was all uphill, though I didn't notice at the time, and unicycles win at going up hills.) We rode the entire 14-mile stretch into Deddington without a break, going faster than 12 miles an hour the whole way.

At this point, I expected I was going to get tired. I didn't. The speed stayed well above 11 miles an hour over the next two legs, with a 30-minute lunch stop in Banbury in the middle. Still feeling fine, with 19 miles to go, I decided to up the speed again. We rode the nine miles into Warwick in 45 minutes.

After a 5-10 minute stop, we were ready to go again. Still feeling fairly energetic, I decided there was no point in riding the final leg slowly. Over the 10 miles from Warwick to Coventry, the speed remained at 13-14 miles an hour, even up the hills. (I overtook Dad on every hill in that leg – there are around six altogether.) Eventually, knees aching, we pulled up outside our house. We had ridden the final 10 miles in just 45 minutes.

Final statistics for the day?

50 miles.

Five hours 15 minutes.

I think Joe was experiencing a rather pronounced surge of testosterone over those weeks. Not only did he keep going on the two major practice rides at much faster speeds than me, but he went on to do two more, equally arduous, rides during the following days. And he was very disparaging of my lack of speed, particularly on uphill sections. It was frustrating that, in spite of all my training, I was struggling to keep up with him. However, we had managed to establish a good rhythm to our rides. Joe would overtake me going uphill, then pause and wait for me at the top, while I would make the most of the downhill sections, regaining my stamina and sometimes allowing myself a bit of momentum to take me up the next incline.

By now, Joe had finished his exams and, with a pending trip to the States to visit a friend, was keen to pack in as much practice as he could. I meanwhile still had a job to do, so left him to his own devices for the next two days.

Joe's Blog:

Yep, the plan was to do London to Brighton and one further ride back to back. But I decided that wasn't challenging enough. Here's what I did:
Day 3: Fifty miles, five hours 10 minutes. Accompanied by my friend Jonnie for the first 10 miles. Solo for the rest of the ride. Very tired by the end.
Day 4: Realised I needed to do a long ride. Seventy miles. Eight and a half hours. Solo.

Really, really sore by the end.

Having packed in the miles in training, Joe flew off to the States, complete with a Kindle, a few clothes and a wash kit, a unicycle, tenor horn and cricket bat all packed in his luggage. He'd gone with two other friends to visit another friend in Madison, Wisconsin. Having finally set the dates and booked the flights, Helen decided to see whether there were any circus skills activities he could participate in while there. In what must be one of the most unusual coincidences in our family life, it turned out that Madison was host to the 2011 North American Unicycling Convention and Championships at exactly the time he was there. So he might have been missing out on further distance practice, but he did get to meet other unicyclists and join in the fun.

CHAPTER 16

The vicar

'You are old, Reverend David,' I said from my bike,
And your beard has grown very long;
And yet you have purchased a recumbent trike –
Don't you think, at your age, that is wrong?'

'In my youth,' Reverend David replied, 'I was glad
To just cycle about on two wheels;
But now, when I think of the speeds to be had –
Why, I'm longing to know how that feels.'

It was sometime after Christmas that we'd gained the third member
of our group: David, our vicar. With the prospect of turning 60
ahead, David decided that an End-to-End cycle ride would be a
good way to celebrate, and asked if we would mind him joining us.
Both Joseph and I thought this would be great, and we could even
see whether others would like to join us to make a small team. Little
did we know, at that stage, just how crucial David's presence in the
team would prove to be.

Somewhere in all the early preparations, David came up with the
idea of doing the ride on a recumbent tricycle, having been inspired
by an article about an elderly Sikh gentleman who'd done just that
the year before. The idea of three generations doing the ride on three
contrasting cycles, with one, two and three wheels respectively,
seemed to appeal to David's sense of aesthetics. So, for his birthday
present, he bought himself a brand new, shiny and sleek tricycle,
earning himself the unique title of the Recumbent Incumbent.

The Recumbent Incumbent – David creeping uphill in the Scottish Highlands

David has not always been a Vicar. He started off his postgraduate working life in residential social work and then, after a further degree in theology, trained as a careers officer. Having completed his probationary period, he set up a workshop for long-term unemployed young people through a parish church outside Sunderland, selling jigsaws to Princess Diana and the young princes amongst others. He then moved into Christian-based community work in inner-city Newcastle. After 15 years living and working with disadvantaged young people and their families, and being fully involved in the political and religious life of the city, he trained for ordained ministry. After ordination, he and Elizabeth continued to live and work in the West End of Newcastle with their three young daughters.

Wikipedia describes Scotswood as a 'dumping ground for less desirable tennents [*sic*] of the city', commenting that it 'was socially destroyed in the early 70's by the local housing counsel [*sic*]'. Whatever the veracity and grammatical accuracy of Wikipedia, it was certainly a challenging place for David and his wife Elizabeth to bring up a young family. They were regularly burgled and now recount with some amusement, though no doubt with some fear at the time, how they woke one morning to find their bedroom window opened more widely than they had left it the night before.

When David got out of bed to close the window, he looked outside and noticed a ladder leaning against the wall. Their garden was totally enclosed and the ladder wasn't theirs. David then saw muddy footprints across the carpet leading to Elizabeth's dressing table. Unbelievably, someone had had the nerve to break into their home while they slept and steal Elizabeth's jewellery. This was in March 1986. Their youngest daughter Hannah was only six weeks old and, as it happens, David's boss from the voluntary organisation Toc H had just stayed that night.

Choosing to live and serve in a deprived urban area is not easy, and it took its toll on David, Elizabeth, and their family. But it also instilled in David an awareness of the very real needs of those who have no choice, of the struggles faced by those living in poverty, and of the realities of trying to work with people in such circumstances. He brought that sense of compassion, coupled with realism, to his work in Coventry. Sensing the potential of a church building right in the heart of the city, and of a church community marked by commitment and a desire to make a difference, he sought to establish Holy Trinity as a 'house of prayer for all': a place and a community where people of all backgrounds can meet with God, without the barriers created by age, ethnicity, language, class or status.

Although, in some ways, David is a reasonably typical Church of England vicar (if there is such a thing), spending three weeks on a journey with him and all the practice beforehand gave us an opportunity to see beyond the Anglican robes. David's Toad-of-Toad-Hall character is, perhaps, summed up very neatly in his approach to cycling.

One of the principles of long-distance cycling is that you work as a team, sticking together, and going at the pace of the slowest. To me, this was crucially important, and an approach I had tried to build in from the start, even on our practice rides. Going uphill, Joe tended to have the edge: with the major advantage of being a very fit, young teenager, and the pressure of a fixed wheel with no gears, he would push himself to keep going at a steady pace till he got to the top. On our practice rides, David and I would struggle up behind and regroup at the top. Going downhill, things were different. Joe, without the stability of two or more wheels, and with no facility for freewheeling, would have to continue at the same, steady pace. Sticking to my principle of staying together, I would regulate my descents, braking gently as I went down, so as not to shoot ahead of Joe. David, too, is very much a team player, valuing and empowering others in their input in the church as on this ride. He did not, however, share my approach of restraining the urge to go shooting ahead when the spirit took him! Having purchased his super-fast tricycle, he was determined to make the most of it, and certainly was not going to be constrained by a slow unicycle when he could zoom down the hills, unencumbered by wind resistance, at speeds of up to 54 mph, aided by the added weight of his bike, baggage and body. Conversely, going uphill David was impeded by the extra weight, and made the most of the luxury permitted by a recumbent tricycle's low centre of gravity, and the ability to stop and apply his handbrake without getting off: he would crawl up at a relatively comfortable pace, pausing to rest as he needed, while Joe would usually go past him, climbing steadily into the distance.

With just over a week to go, there still seemed to be a lot to prepare for this challenge. Things were coming together though. While Joe was away in the States, I cycled 80 miles from Coventry to Newark, to join a group from our church at the New Wine Christian conference. It was a perfect day for it, and, having woken early, I set out just after six am. The route through North Warwickshire, trailing the Coventry then Ashby canals, was stunning. And that early on a Sunday morning, it was peaceful and traffic-free. From the delightful village of Heather, where the annual scarecrow festival (yes honestly!) was just getting going, I cut across through Coalville, Whitwick and Thringstone, and past Osgathorpe (England boasts some wonderful place-names) to Belton. From there, I crossed over to Zouch, the Leakes, Bunny and Cropwell Bishop, before heading north through Aslockton and Thoroton to finish along the disused railway line into Newark.

The conference was excellent: a great chance to relax, socialise with others from our church, catch up on some reading, and be inspired by some challenging talks and seminars. Many of the young children from our church were practising their cycling skills, and I thought it would be good if we could get one of the youngsters, Sam, to join us on his little bike with stabilisers, to complete the theme of one wheel, two wheels, three wheels, and then four wheels. On reflection, I decided that wasn't such a good idea: he might have struggled to keep up over that kind of distance and I'm not sure what his parents would have thought.

David had brought his tricycle, and several of us had goes riding it up and down the disused runway on site. He and I did two good practice rides, one up to Donnington Hall and back, then the second, from Shardlow to Newark, after dropping off our car for a service. The latter ended up being rather longer than I anticipated (48 miles rather than 35) and was partly in the rain, but together both were helpful in putting David's tricycle through its paces.

The conference over, we all returned to Coventry, and suddenly the ride seemed ominously close. Joe, back from the States, threw himself into helping with the Spark in the Park holiday club; I was back at work; David had his parish duties to put in order; Helen and Elizabeth were planning the menu and support arrangements; and we were all going backwards and forwards sorting out the final preparations. Meanwhile the support and encouragements kept coming in. We managed to exceed our £6,000 target before we'd even begun, and in a rash moment, I decided to double that to £12,000. Joe's blog for that week captured some of the activity of that week, and also hinted at the nervousness that we were all now feeling:

'Spark Free!' reads the sign on the side of the Marquee.

Yes, we are trying to avoid any fires. But what the sign aims to communicate is that Spark in the Park is now happening in Coventry. With a few days of reasonably good weather, we have apparently had record numbers of families in the park (over 500 each day). This means we've also needed huge numbers of helpers. Running activities during the day, and continuing supervising activities in the evening, we're all exhausted, but enjoying it.

I've been helping out with sports for most of the time, with occasional breaks to wander around on stilts, or do a bit of balloon modelling. (At the Spark disco this evening, I made my craziest balloon model yet – a giant duck-billed platypus, needing 10 balloons to make, and taking over an hour

– I had no instructions.) So with all this going on, I haven't had much chance for training in the final week. But it doesn't matter too much – it's good to have a break from training just before the ride.

So the ride is on Sunday. I'm nervous. I'm also not entirely sure that doubling our sponsorship target was a good idea. But hey.

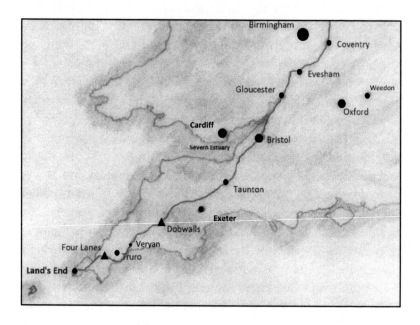

Map 3: Land's End to Coventry

CHAPTER 17

Land's End

Joe's Blog, 14th August, 2011:

A Chinese proverb, quoted by Dad, states that 'even the longest journey starts with a single step'. Or something along those lines. In this case, naturally, 'step' is replaced by 'turn of the wheel'. Unfortunately, it was a turn of the car wheels, as we had to get to Land's End before we could start riding. This meant waking up at half past five. Leaving Coventry at around ten to seven this morning, we eventually reached Land's End shortly before two. After unloading the cycles, getting ready and having photos etc., we were ready to leave by three. A great crowd of people ready to send us off – one of my friends from Bristol, who happened to be on holiday in Cornwall, had brought his extended family along to see us start. In total, 16 people plus Neo, the dog. Also, the Lord Mayor of Coventry, who gave us a countdown via the phone.

So, we started. The very first rotations of our six wheels. One thousand, one hundred and forty-five miles still to be covered.

For me, the realisation kicked in about four miles into the ride – a great excitement at the fact that we had finally started, after the months of preparation.

We couldn't have asked for a better start: warm and sunny, though not too hot; a gentle, westerly breeze blowing, and perfect views over the sea to Longships Lighthouse, and the Scillies beyond. As Joe pointed out, this was 'one of the nicest routes we've done for a while', along the coast to Sennen cove, then inland on quiet Cornish lanes, through the little villages of Buryan and Lamorna, to the beautiful harbour at Mousehole. We passed several ancient stone crosses, standing stones and the Merry Maidens stone circle near St Buryan. The finest stone was the Boskenna Cross, with a worn but still recognisable carving of the crucified Christ. It was mounted on a circular stone, with a carved groove and rim at the base. David wondered whether that might have been used for pouring water for baptism, but I found out later that it was actually the base of a not-so-old cider press! Perhaps more in keeping with a 'water-into-wine', party-loving Jesus than a camel-hair shirt, 'repent and be baptised' John.

The Start – Three enthusiastic cyclists and over 1,000 miles to go

Mousehole was in the midst of a carnival, so there was plenty of activity, including one pirate offering 'children's heads chopped off for free'. But we didn't see any evidence that anyone had taken him up on this.

After Mousehole, we experienced some more recent history in the remnants of tin mines. We passed some fascinating workings, both on the first evening and the following morning. At Gwinear, I spotted a delightful epitaph:

Henry Hendra, died 14th July, 1819, aged 35 years. He was an honest, sober and industrious miner, whose constant attendance within these sacred walls at the hours of public worship procured him the distinguishing epithet of 'the churchman'.

I suspect most Cornish miners were not known for their sobriety or spirituality. But I also suspect that most were both honest and industrious. And perhaps an honest, industrious drunkard is closer to God's heart than a straight-faced but hypocritical churchman.

Joe's audio-diary:

We've stopped for a brief pause at Gwinear, where St Gwinear's parish church is celebrating its 750th anniversary. And David, meanwhile, is trying to unjam his chain. Helen is at the campsite putting everything up.

A bit later:

Still waiting by the church in Gwinear. Dad's gone back down the hill to help David with the tricycle. Don't envy him having to get back up the hill again, at all; but he seemed happy enough to do it, and the tricycle definitely needs fixing.

Still later:

I've been in Gwinear for nearly half an hour now and the rather raucous and persistent sound of some crows in the trees above is the only sound I've heard, pretty much. There aren't really any people around, and so I'm just free to wait for David, and listen to the birds making this racket. It really is quite impressive.

Another entry:

I've now been in Gwinear 40 minutes. Dad and David have just fixed the chain, so should be coming up here shortly. Still no let-up from the birds. In fact, if anything, they've got more noisy. It's getting slightly on the annoying side now. I certainly wouldn't like to live here. Hopefully be on our way soon and in the campsite in about an hour.

A final recording from Joe:

Fifty minutes, and David's reached the top of the hill.

Shortly after that enforced break, a great milestone was reached, with Joe's speedometer registering a total distance of 1,000 miles – mostly made up of practice rides, but quite an achievement in itself. A few miles later and we rolled into the Four Lanes campsite at Lanyon Farm. Thirty-four miles in five hours – not the best start timing-wise. And David's trike was definitely in need of attention.

We realised however that we were not far from Falmouth, where ICE Trikes, from whom David had bought the tricycle, were located. So the following morning, he and Helen drove down there and got it fixed. Being a good vicar, David saw an excellent sermon brewing here – something along the lines of the advantages of being close to the Creator when things go wrong! The guys at ICE Trikes, like Roger at Unicycle.com, are enthusiasts. Building and selling these machines is not just a job, but a passion. So they were keen to have a look, diagnose the problem, and get it sorted. It seemed to be a mixture of mechanical and human error, with a deliberate inbuilt design flaw.

The tricycle – a miracle of modern engineering

The tricycle is, in fact, quite a miracle of modern engineering, and way beyond my conceptual powers to fully understand. It has an incredibly long chain stretching from the pedals out in front, to the driving wheel behind. This chain not only needs to respond to the varying lengths required by changing gears, but also to adjustments to the boom according to the leg length of the rider, and a neat folding mechanism, which allows the trike to be bent in half for transport. With such long, hidden stretches of chain, it is easy to introduce a twist, and this in fact was what had happened when it was first assembled from its flat-pack, so that it ended up 180° out of sync. Then there is the question of technique. Unlike a bicycle, it is quite possible on the tricycle, being stable on three wheels, to roll gently backwards on a slope without falling over. It seems that, if you try to change gear while doing so, the chain will not run true, and in this case, managed to jump over the innermost cog, getting jammed between the gears and the spokes of the wheel. David eventually mastered the technique of only changing gear when he had sufficient forward momentum (somewhere in the depths of Scotland, having covered around 850 miles, David came out with the impressive statement that, 'I think I'm getting the hang of these gears'!). But that early on in the ride, he was still getting used to his machine; the chain ended up well and truly jammed, and the tricycle came to a grinding halt. That's where the inbuilt design flaw came in handy. Because of the stresses involved, a sudden halt could very easily end up damaging the main frame of the tricycle. That, clearly, would be a very expensive malady. So, to protect the main frame, the makers had built in a relatively weak bracket on the gearing system. This bracket was designed to buckle under stress, and so it did.

Joe's audio diary, Sunday evening, 14th August:

In terms of my thoughts about the ride so far, they haven't changed that much since this morning to be honest. I've got over the initial excitement of the fact that we've started and just got down to normal riding now, which I suspect I'll be doing for rather a large amount of the ride; but still enjoying it. It's been a nice ride today. A few more hills than I would have liked, but that's not particularly surprising in Cornwall. It's a bit chilly now, but the weather's still good. And, yeah, it's been a good ride.

It had been a good ride for me too. Feeling more fit and energetic after all our practice rides, with the route sorted, and the sponsorship flooding in, I had got over my initial reservations about accompanying Joe. I was looking forward to these next three weeks – to the chance to see something of Britain's amazing and varied scenery, from the sharp, hedgerowed lanes of Cornwall and Devon, the heights of Dartmoor, to the flat plains of Somerset, the gentle leafy Midland shires, and on to the wilder expanses of Northumbria and the Scottish Highlands. I was keenly anticipating the exhilaration of some challenging rides at the peak of my fitness, and the opportunities to be with Joe and to get to know David more. As we sat down together outside the tents to share a meal of pasta and a glass of wine, I knew we were in for a good three weeks, that not even the vagaries of the tricycle's mechanics could spoil.

CHAPTER 18

The stroke

It was our second day of cycling. We'd got off to a slow start following the problems with the tricycle, but had made good progress, and were more or less back on track. After a lovely pub lunch in Philleigh, we dropped down once more to the coast at Pendower Beach, where we had to push our cycles along the sand for a bit. We then had a very steep climb up again towards Veryan. We'd been joined for the day by one of David's relatives, Mark, on his new road bike; and he, Joe, and I all got off and pushed our cycles up, taking it very gently. Even Joe, the fit, young member of our team, had found it necessary to dismount and push his unicycle up the hill.

We paused at the top to regroup, and it was while we were waiting for David to cycle up that I noticed the vision in my left eye was blurred – a sort of greyish mist across the centre, as though someone had taken some dilute paint and brushed across my view. I assumed this would go away after a while, so sat down for a bit. As it hadn't cleared by the time David had reached us I thought we could set off, in the hope that it would gradually resolve once we got going. Standing up again with my bike though didn't work, and I had to rather hastily sit and then lie down, feeling far from normal.

There ensued a series of intriguing changes. I assumed this was a transient thing that would hopefully clear up quickly so we could get on with the ride. It was eminently clear, however, to the rest of the team, that something was seriously wrong. As David, then Helen on the phone, then the ambulance crew, asked me various questions, it was rather strange understanding everything, knowing exactly what I wanted to reply, but being totally unable to say the words. Even more unusual was realising, when the ambulance crew asked me to raise my right arm, that I couldn't do so; indeed, I think I had been quite oblivious to the presence of my right arm till then. I was quite entertained by being able to lift my arm with my left hand then let it drop back, lifeless, beside me.

Poor Joseph and Helen, I think, had the worst of this: Joe, having an uncomfortable ride through narrow Cornish lanes in the back of an ambulance with an incoherent father; and Helen, who had managed to glean a few incoherent words from me, and a worried comment from Joe that 'Dad doesn't look good', before the mobile reception went, leaving her completely in the dark, with little idea as to whether or not I was even alive. Helen later recorded her impression of the events in her journal:

On the outskirts of Redruth got a call from David saying Peter wasn't well and he thought we should collect him. Hmm… what sort of not well? 'Does he need an ambulance?' 'No, you can talk to him.' David passed the phone over. 'Hi, how are you doing? What's going on?' All I got was 'yeah' in a slurred voice. 'Peter, what's the matter?' 'Yeah.' 'Peter, pass the phone to David so he can call an ambulance.' Then silence. The phone went dead. We set off to drive to where we thought they were, me praying and trying not to panic. After a while we managed to get Joe on Peter's mobile. Joe said an ambulance had been called, but 'Dad's not looking good.' I asked if he was lying down and told Joe to put him in the recovery position and check he was still breathing. I was about to say, 'if he stops breathing start CPR', but the line went again. We carried on driving, then I tried the phone again and got Joe, in the ambulance, saying Dad was still confused but alive! We turned and headed towards the hospital, having seen the ambulance drive past us. The next phone call from Joe was a heart-stopper: in his most serious voice, 'Mum, we got to the hospital about 15 minutes ago and Dad's…' I was waiting for the words I dreaded, 'and Dad's dead'. When Joe finally managed to say, 'Dad's having a scan', I breathed a huge sigh of relief. What if Peter had been dead on arrival, or died soon after? What if I hadn't been there for Joe?

Ally, the nurse consultant with the stroke unit, was absolutely amazing – making sure the junior A&E doctor did all the right things; looking after me; taking Joe under her wing until Helen arrived; and with a wonderful calm, confident air, ensuring that I got the very best care the NHS had to offer. It was only as I was being assessed by the doctor, and wheeled off for my CT scan, that it gradually dawned on me that I'd had a stroke; and that this might have fairly major implications for our ride.

Over the next few hours it became clear that this was, in fact, a less severe event called a TIA (Transient Ischaemic Attack); although, as one of my colleagues pointed out in an email, 'you don't know that it is a TIA until you know it's not a stroke'.[1]

I then had the equally intriguing, but far more positive, experience of observing my body start functioning again, in more or less reverse order to the loss. While I was having my CT scan, my right hand suddenly started moving again. I felt like a young infant, discovering for the first time that this object with five digits sticking off it is actually something he can move and control. As my strength gradually returned, I revelled in opening and clenching my fist, then raising my arm up in the air, and reaching out to touch Joe and Helen. My speech, too, gradually returned, so I was able to talk sense once again. Later that evening, carefully watched by two nurses, I took my first walk down the ward. My vision took longest to recover, but by the evening was completely clear again.

In spite of this quick recovery, it was becoming clear that I wouldn't be able to jump straight back on my bike the next day. We contemplated calling the whole thing off, but after various discussions with all involved, Joe decided that he would like to carry on. We decided, therefore, that the best thing would be for Joe and David to continue with the journey rather than wait for me to recover. All being well, I would be able to take a few days out with Helen and Elizabeth in the support car, then rejoin the lads once I'd regained my strength.

---

[1] A TIA is essentially the same as a stroke, with a part of the brain being deprived of oxygen, resulting in a loss of function in part of the body. However, by definition, with a TIA all function returns to normal within 24 hours, whereas with a stroke, the symptoms persist for longer.

So it was that the following day – a damp, grey Tuesday morning – a rather subdued but determined unicyclist and vicar resumed their epic journey; while I, a subdued, but still determined, paediatrician, started out on a rather different and unexpected journey.

CHAPTER 19

The road to Paradise

Joe's blog, 16th August:

We set out at around 10:30 this morning. Firstly riding back to where we left off yesterday, then taking a slightly modified route up towards the Eden Project. David's friend Mark was still with us, getting significantly more riding than yesterday.

We got into St Austell without too much trouble. A fairly large hill going down into St Austell where David managed to set a new top speed record of 46 mph, breaking the 40 mph speed limit as he did so. A slight debate over the route in St Austell, but we eventually found it and headed up towards the Eden project. About half a mile away from the Eden project we had a long stop because the gears on David's trike mucked up again. Thankfully we stopped just outside a warehouse, where there happened to be a couple of cycle mechanics. So we took the wheel off, switched over one of the parts, and were on our way again.

As we came towards the Eden Project there was a very nice view looking down into the Eden valley. We could see all the domed roofs, which were very impressive from where we were. Down there was the car park where I had the rest of my Cornish pastie, while David cycled round the car park for no particular reason, and we let Mark go and join his family. It's been great cycling with Mark. His speed has generally been somewhere between mine and David's; slower than David downhill, faster than David uphill, and, obviously, vice-versa for me. It has been very helpful having him along, especially with the slight mishaps we've had. Anyway, we left him there at the Eden Project, and pressed on.

'The Road to Paradise' (Paradise here represented by Eden) came to an abrupt end, with a mammoth hill up out of St Blazey. When I say

mammoth, I mean it. It was really ridiculously long. It took me ages to get up, and David even longer – I was waiting for him for nine minutes at the top in the end. Anyway, from there, it was up along the A-road for a fairly long way into Lostwithiel.

My plans to visit the Eden Project had been shattered. I had never been there, and had assumed that, with an early start on day two, and just 50 miles cycling, we could stop there for a break, joining Helen and Elizabeth, who would have been able to spend even longer looking round, between striking camp and setting up at the next site. All that was not to be and my visit to Eden will have to wait for another time.

Built 10 years ago in a disused clay mine, the whole ethos of Eden captures so much of what I strive for in my life, and, in a series of transparent domes, seems to encapsulate a vision of a renewed world. Their expressed aims, highlighted on their website (www.edenproject.com), seem to echo a gospel of regeneration, justice and hope:

- *People and learning: We aim to inspire people about their world, foster their talents and help them to connect with each other in new ways.*
- *Places and regeneration: We're working on projects worldwide that bring about environmental, social, economic regeneration.*
- *Climate and environment: As well as running Eden in the greenest way we can, we invite the public and business to engage with these issues.*
- *Plants and gardens: We show visitors how important plants are; we also use gardening as a way of empowering disengaged people.*
- *Music and art: Our rich programme of events excite and engage people to show that, together, we can make amazing things happen.*

Whichever way you look at it, this world is not perfect. I'm not convinced it ever was: even the most literal interpreters of the Bible have to accept that Genesis refers to God seeing all that he had made as 'good', even 'very good'; but not 'perfect'. And what we observe of our world now is certainly far from perfect. Alongside the inherent beauty of awe-inspiring views, stunning sunsets, peaceful hideaways, there is also the terrifying reality of crashing tsunamis, earthquakes, famine and drought. Hand-in-hand with the most remarkable achievements of civilisation – penicillin, the bicycle, a decent cappuccino, Rachmaninov's Second Piano Concerto – are the violence, greed, pride and hypocrisy that leave others wounded and oppressed, and have gouged deep scars into the very fabric of our world. And yet, through all this messed-up confusion, there are signs of hope and beauty. In the words of one of my favourite songs[2]:

> *There's a lot of pain, but a lot more healing*
> *There's a lot of trouble, but a lot more peace*
> *There's a lot of hate but a lot more loving…*
> *There's a lot of darkness, but a lot more light.*

And so, while Eden remains a future hope, we were able to see beauty in the British countryside, and in the lives of people we met on our journey. However, for me, that dream was shattered. While David and Joe pressed on through Cornwall, I was trapped in a ward in Truro Hospital. My longings to visit Eden and be inspired in its domes, to take in the awesome beauty of Bodmin Moor, to meet with ordinary English folk on our way were all shelved. Instead of immersing myself in the richness of these experiences, I would need to content myself with reading Joe's blogs and listening to his audio descriptions on the Dictaphone I'd given him. In typical teenage fashion, Joe was given to somewhat understating things, referring to my TIA as a 'slight mishap', and summing up Bodmin Moor as having 'some very nice scenery', focusing instead on what was more important to him as a teenage unicyclist with a long journey ahead:

In Lostwithiel, the idea was that we left the A-road and headed up past the castle. But, after cycling up a fairly long hill, we discovered that the route didn't exist, so sadly, we had to turn around and cycle all the way back down into Lostwithiel. And then cycle back up out of it along the A-road, which

---

[2]   Godfrey Birtill, 'Outrageous Grace'. Copyright ©2000 Thank You Music

wasn't too much fun. We continued along the A-road and eventually got into the campsite shortly before six o'clock. This, of course, was the campsite where we were meant to be at the end of day two. We had a quick bite to eat there. David had his pastie from earlier and a cup of tea; I had two bowls of cereal, and we were on our way again, trying to go as far as we could before we got picked up.

We had a lovely route up over Bodmin Moor, heading towards Upton Cross. I was really enjoying it actually. It was uphill quite a lot, but still very nice. There were some beautiful views at the top, and a couple of strange landmarks. There was the stone of king someone or other. He'd been a Cornish king in the late ninth century, and ordered two stones put up with crosses on them, for the preservation of his soul; and sadly, later, was drowned. Ah well, I'm sure his soul was preserved very well! [This was King Doniert's Stone by St Cleer – two elaborately carved stones probably dating from the late ninth century.]

A little further on up the hill we found out that Bodmin Moor is a national World Heritage site, and an area of outstanding natural beauty. And it certainly was some very nice scenery up there. Back down the other side of Bodmin Moor, which wasn't quite as much fun for me, but still not too bad. I was making good use of the brake, and David, obviously, ahead of me, but not too far ahead; then down through Bray Cross where we stopped to phone Mum.

There was obviously no sense in waiting around to be picked up, so we decided to press on towards Horsebridge, a further four miles. When we got there, we had a very nice surprise, in that we'd reached the border of Devon. We were planning to stop there, but after five minutes of waiting around for Mum to arrive, we decided to press on a bit further, because there was apparently a four-mile-long hill up out of Horsebridge. Not looking forward to that too much, so we decided to get started. We rode up, it must have been about a quarter of a mile, and then got interrupted by the arrival of the Galaxy. It was very nice to stop, and, thankfully, we'll have a bit less of that four mile hill to do tomorrow.

So, we have officially reached Devon. Sixty miles today, around 10 hours. Still more than 30 miles behind.

The cyclists reach Devon – 30 miles behind schedule, but back on the road

CHAPTER 20

The stroke ward

Hannah's Dad: 'Esther's Dad has had a TIA.'
Hannah (wondering what a TIA is): 'Oh, that's nice!'
Hannah's Dad: 'Um, no, not nice.'
Hannah: 'Right. Err, what's a TIA?'

In the days following my TIA, I received loads of heart-felt encouraging emails and blog comments from friends and colleagues all over the country. I discovered that at least four of my colleagues had had similar experiences. Two of them have since been back running marathons, so that gave a lot of hope for a full recovery. It subsequently transpired that the TIA had been caused by a carotid artery dissection – a small tear in the wall of my left carotid artery. The consultant told me that these dissections typically seem to affect fit, active, young men. So I have milked that for all it's worth – it is official now: in spite of my TIA, I am fit, active and young!

I was indeed the youngest person on the ward, and the following day, while Joe and David pressed on through Paradise, I took great delight in wandering down the ward in my cycling shorts and top (those being the only clothes I had with me, and far more comfortable than the standard hospital gown). The others in the four-bedded bay into which I was wheeled that afternoon had a much harder time; but even in the short period of time I was with them, it seemed as though we built up a kind of camaraderie. Viv, in the bed next to me, was a retired PE teacher to whom I warmed immediately. We quickly found that we had a lot in common, including a love of the outdoors; a shared Christian faith; inspiration from running church youth groups; and most of all, a deep love for our respective families, about whom we were able to talk with each other, and shed a few emotional tears. Viv, who was far more fit and active than me, and a very keen cyclist, was suffering from Guillain-Barré syndrome (an unusual condition which results in progressive, but usually transient, muscle weakness, that can be severe enough to require intensive care treatment if the respiratory muscles are affected). Being stuck in a hospital bed and unable to get up and walk was, of course, extremely frustrating for someone who would much rather be cycling around Cornwall at ridiculous speeds. The other two, Donald, an 82-year-old Cornish farmer, and John, a sprightly 89-year-old from Peterborough, had both suffered strokes and were in the early stages of rehabilitation, with a long, slow road to recovery ahead.

John, who had a nice little sense of humour, seemed to take quite a fancy to all the attractive young nurses who were looking after us. He managed to puzzle a young Filipina bank nurse by telling her that he once had a Filipina girlfriend called Imelda. I think she wasn't quite sure whether or not to take him seriously until he went on to say that his girlfriend had 3,000 pairs of shoes.

Although the actual number of shoes was probably closer to 1,000, Imelda Marcos' extravagant collection became an obscene icon of greed and corruption when so many of her fellow Filipinos lived, and continue to live, in abject poverty.

In 2004, Joe, Esther and I had the privilege of visiting the Philippines and spending a few days with the family of Pastor Wenchi, in a Manila slum, while Helen was busy with meetings nearby. Pastor Wenchi, his wife and four children, lived in a two-roomed house on top of a school building in the middle of an area called Project 8. The family graciously moved into one room so we could have the other, a six-foot-square room with a comfortable mattress but little else. Over four days they shared their home, their food and their lives with us. Out of so little, their generosity, both to us, and to their neighbours in the slum, shone like a light.

I have seen that time and time again in my visits to Asia, and in a way we can hardly dream of here. I have been welcomed into people's homes – Efren and Becky, Orr-Ee, Hem Neang; and have drunk tea with people for whom a Starbuck's latte may represent a whole week's food budget. Slums are horrible places – dirty, dark, rank, and with violence, hardship and sickness rife; but they are also places of beauty, where hospitality, friendship and laughter abound.

You don't have to go to the other side of the world, however, to experience hardship and suffering. Nor to experience kindness and hope. I saw both during my brief stay in Truro Hospital. For Viv, the frustration of being confined to a hospital ward was at times almost more than he could bear. John, separated from his wife, and longing to be transferred to Peterborough Hospital, had his moments of tears. And Donald seemed at times despairing of ever getting back to his beloved farm. And yet, for all of us, there were little rays of life: the nursing staff who were gentle and caring, and ever-so patient, in spite of heavy workloads; the cleaners who stopped to talk and laugh with us; the therapists who inspired us to keep looking forward. Having seen it now from the other side, I am more convinced than ever that the NHS is one of the most wonderful institutions in the world, and the staff who work in it do the most tremendous jobs.

Having said that, hospital wards are not good places for peace and rest. So, when I was told the following morning that I would be able to leave, I was thoroughly relieved. The night had passed slowly. By the time the nurses had finished the late-night drug round, it was after 11. They were just preparing to turn out the main ward lights, and I was looking forward to finally getting some decent rest, when the consultant appeared, to clerk me in. In spite of the late hour, and no doubt a long day for her, she was caring and thorough in her history-taking, examination and management. She decided it would be best to start me on heparin and statins, and being so late, I wasn't prepared to argue, or to ask for the latest evidence of their effectiveness from randomised controlled trials. So I acquiesced and submitted myself to a subcutaneous injection and a further tablet. Then, finally, Viv was helped back into bed, and the lights went out. Peace, however, did not descend.

Between the four of us, I think we managed quite a chorus of snoring at different points in the night. Most frustrating, though, was Donald's high-tech air bed. Designed to prevent pressure sores by sending pulses of air through the mattress, it was another miracle of modern engineering, and vitally important for someone in his position with limited movement. The alarm system, however, was not working properly, so every 20 minutes or so, we would be treated to 72 high-pitched beeps until it settled down again. That doesn't promote sleep.

I think, in spite of that, I must have at least dozed off a bit, because I was woken at around three am to a loud crash beside me. Viv had woken in the night, and forgetting where he was and what was wrong with him, had tried to get out of bed to go to the loo. As he got out of bed his legs gave way beneath him, so I woke to find him kneeling on the floor and totally unable to get back into bed. After checking he was OK, I went off to find the nurses who were busy down the other end of the ward, so hadn't been able to come immediately when I pressed the alarm buzzer. They got a hoist and got Viv back into bed, but while they were doing so, John, too, woke up disorientated, and decided he would try to go off to the loo. Fortunately he didn't get as far as the loo before we spotted him, and one of the nurses was able to get him settled again.

The rest of the night passed uneventfully, and the following morning I was whisked off for an ultrasound scan and the MRI scan that showed the carotid dissection. Again, the NHS proved itself to be efficient and caring, with friendly porters, technicians and radiographers, all excelling at their jobs.

That afternoon I saw the stroke consultant who explained that carotid dissections generally heal themselves, and just require treatment with low-dose aspirin to prevent blood clots forming, plus avoidance of strenuous exercise for a time. So, that put paid to any hopes of rejoining the cycle ride before the end. But, at least it meant I could leave the hospital and rejoin Helen for one night camping before heading home for some more substantial rest.

Helen, after a good 24 hours of worry, summed up her relief in her journal:

After picking up Peter and setting up the campsite, Joe phoned up to be collected at Horsebridge. I headed off in the car, leaving Peter resting and Elizabeth clearing up supper. It was dark by then and we got back to the campsite at around nine pm. Food, shower, and bed! Still, it was amazing just to lie in my sleeping bag and have Peter alive beside me.

CHAPTER 21

Pressing on

The following day, Helen dropped David and Joe off at Horsebridge. It was another late start, but they pressed on and managed about 75 miles via Okehampton, Crediton and Tiverton, getting to the outskirts of Taunton after dark. But that's jumping ahead a bit.

Joe's audio diary, 17th August:

I'm tired. Just stopped for a breather at the top of a very large hill waiting for David to catch up. It's the start of the fourth day of riding. We're now into the hills of Devon, rather than Cornwall, but they don't seem to be a huge amount better at the moment. It's raining fairly lightly, so not too bad as far as the weather is concerned. We're trying to push on a bit and reach Taunton today, which should enable us to be back on schedule tomorrow.

Just briefly reflecting on the annoyingness of hills. Especially several of the ones we've been going along at the moment. They have an annoying habit of levelling off, so that you think they've finished, and then, when you get there, it turns out that they haven't, and it's actually another half-k to the top. And then you ride half a k, and you find out it's just another brief levelling off and you've still got to go further to reach the top. And it's getting rather irritating to say the least.

Later:

Fairly nice morning's riding in the rain. We've now done between eight and nine miles. We're at the bottom of Lydford Gorge, which claims to be the deepest gorge in the South West. This is slightly worrying when you consider that we've got to ride up the other side. But, oh well, I'm sure we'll have fun doing that. Hopefully we'll get to Lydford soon.

A message from Nick and Alison, adding to the huge list of supportive comments we've had regarding Dad. That's been very helpful over the past few days.

Later that afternoon:

Well, we opted to stay on the A-road for a bit, rather than going straight onto the cycle path, which may well have been a good decision. We made reasonable speed on there, despite the hills. We've now come onto the cycle path. It's the Granite Way into Okehampton, and it's a very nice stretch along here: very nice riding. David's shooting past me on his trike, and we should be in Okehampton soon.

Incredible views coming over Meldon viaduct. Wish I could stop to take a picture, but I can't. I'll just say it for the record, 'very, very nice'.

Just having a brief stop at a cycle shop in Okehampton, while David gets his gears fixed, and also a problem with his mudguard. All seems fairly simple, so hopefully should be on our way shortly. We've now done 20 miles, and it's quarter past two, so we've still been going quite slowly, but it's not too bad at the moment. Might make it into Taunton by nine o'clock; I'm not entirely sure; it will largely depend on the hills.

Just got to the top of a rather large hill outside Okehampton, called Appledore Hill according to the map. I'll just wait a bit for David to catch up. Fairly nice views at the top; it would be better if there weren't quite so many hedges. But still, can very clearly see all the hills we've just come over, which is quite nice. Hopefully not too many more today. We're hoping to do another 20-30 miles before we stop for supper.

A very nice blue dragonfly just in front of me here. In fact it's quite a nice corner, as corners go. I'm just waiting at a junction at the top of a very large hill before Crediton. It's the longest we've had for quite a while. And, if Dad's right, we shouldn't have anything of this scale for a very long time. He said most of the hills were before Crediton, so it should hopefully be a significantly easier ride afterwards. It's half-four, and when we get into Crediton, we'll have done between 35 and 40 miles. So, we've been fairly slow, which isn't particularly surprising due to the hills. But hopefully not too bad, and, as I said, hopefully should speed up after Crediton.

After seeing Joe and David off again, through Devon, we packed up the camp (or rather Helen and Elizabeth packed up, while I sat about reading and composing an email to all my friends and colleagues to let them know what had happened). Over the ensuing days, and even more so when I rejoined the support crew for the final leg up into Scotland, I came to appreciate the incredible resilience and fortitude of Helen, who somehow managed to keep the whole thing together.

As we were planning the journey, I had rather naively thought that this could be an enjoyable trip for Helen too. I realised there would be hard work, but had assumed that, once she had packed up the camp each morning, she would have time to take Neo for a nice walk somewhere, then move on to the next campsite and, having put up the tents, would be able to relax with a cup of tea and a book while she waited for the cyclists to get in. The reality was very different. Even without the emotional turmoil of my hospital admission and subsequent slow recovery, Helen had, I think, the hardest job of all. Setting up and packing away a campsite for the whole team, mostly single-handed, while also driving back and forth, checking on the progress of the riders, seeking out and delivering spare parts, snacks and other essentials, and coping with all the little (and large) incidents that served to complicate the venture. It seemed as though everything was stacked against us. Not only had I suffered my unexpected illness, but as a team we had to cope with mechanical failure, difficulties with the route, long days with late nights and a whole host of little problems. Through it all, it seemed that Helen was the one stabilising influence, without which I have no doubt the whole challenge would have collapsed.

Joe's audio diary, late afternoon, 17th August:

Just stopped and met up with the support crew shortly after Crediton, where David had fish and chips and I had my lunch. Still trying to push on and reach Taunton. Hopefully only about 25 miles now, and also, hopefully, slightly flatter, though it isn't looking too promising from where I am.

Oh, my goodness. Oh dear. Um, yeah. I've just reached the top of a ridiculously big hill, somewhere between Crediton and Tiverton. I'm not exactly sure where. I crawled up the majority of it at about five mph and it took me 15 minutes, so it is a stupidly long hill. But, at the same time, I made it all the way up, which, to be perfectly honest, I'm rather pleased with. Thankfully, I'm going to get a bit of a break before David makes it to the top. And, yep, that certainly won't have helped us speed up the pace at all. No views from the top as of yet. I'm rather surrounded by trees. But as I was coming up, I had a very nice view off to my right of… nothing. Meaning that, over to the east at any rate, the country is essentially flat. Hopefully, it will be similar in the direction we're going. I really, really hope so. If it is, we might just make it to the end of the day at a reasonable time. This will certainly be a very good hill to finish the hilly stretch on. Definitely the longest one we've done so far. Oh dear.

Later:

We're just cycling along the Grand Western Canal at the moment, which, aside from being very picturesque, is also very flat, which makes a change from the hills of earlier in the morning. The only downside is that it's currently ten past eight and we've got 18 miles to ride. A slight mistake on Dad's part working out the route. It's 77 miles from Horsebridge to Taunton, rather than 67 as he thought. So, we're going to be a while longer; it's looking like we'll be getting into the B&B after 10 at this rate. Not too good, but at least we should make it. Hopefully, if we get up early tomorrow, we can still make the 80 miles into Gloucester. Anyway, as I said, it's nice and flat, so we're putting on a reasonable bit of speed along the canal, hoping to move onto the A-road soon, to take us the rest of the way into Taunton.

On leaving the Great Western Canal, or whatever it's called, we were routed by a rather large hill. Nothing on the scale of the earlier ones, but still quite a shock. It's been our first hill, basically, since Tiverton now. The sun has very nearly set now, it's a fairly nice sunset, but yeah, it's now getting pretty dark. It's ten to nine and we've still potentially got another 10 miles to go to reach Taunton. So, it looks like we're going to be riding along the A38 for a bit in the dark. I'm fairly sure I can see the A38 just down there, so we should be joining that very shortly. And then we'll see what happens.

The back of my knee is rubbing a little bit. I think I'll need to sort that out tomorrow, 'cause I certainly don't want to ride another 80 miles like that. The brace, however, has helped; my knee seems to be holding out very well. I'm rather on the tired side, and it doesn't look like I'll be getting any supper, which probably isn't too good to be honest. But, hopefully, will still manage to find enough energy for tomorrow. Oh dear.

We reached Taunton after 10. Very scary riding along the A38 in the dark, but a very nice B&B at the end to make up for it.

Our aim was to book David and Joe into a hotel or B&B for the night, while we headed back to Coventry, so I could rest at home for a few days, and we could be with Esther for her A-level results. After a lot of driving round Taunton, we managed to find a lovely bed and breakfast, where the proprietor, Barbara, was very helpful and made the two of them very comfortable. We left some pasta for Joe to stock up on when they arrived, and set off, arriving in Coventry around midnight and tumbling into our beds.

Perhaps not surprisingly, both Helen and I felt quite emotional after getting back to Coventry – I think the stress of the past few days finally caught up with us. We felt a bit like the hobbits in *The Lord of the Rings*, with Helen, Elizabeth and I whisked off to Coventry, while Joe and David, like Frodo and Sam, battled on through rough terrain and inclement weather. It was good to be at home, although very frustrating not to be cycling with Joe and David, who made excellent progress, in spite of heavy rain, through Somerset and Bristol, and carrying on into Gloucestershire.

Joe's Blog, 18th August:

The plan was to ride 80 miles up to Gloucester, bringing us back on schedule. This seemed like it was going out of the window when we discovered it was nearly 50 miles into Bristol. However, the route was flat, and along the A38. Rather wet, but we coped, reaching Bristol after three. Here we met up with Brian, an old friend from Bristol, who was vitally important guiding us through the centre and onto the A38 towards Gloucester.

We left Brian shortly after leaving Bristol, then pushed on up the A38. Incredibly, we were on the outskirts of Gloucester by about 7:30. Brian picked us up in his van, and we headed back to his house in Bristol for the night.

Statistics – Over 80 miles covered, in around 10 hours. (David makes it 83.) Average riding speed around 11 miles an hour. Distance to Coventry: 50-60 miles. Distance behind schedule around five miles.

After a restful night in Bristol, Brian dropped Joe and David off again where they'd finished the previous evening, and they carried on, making good speed, all the way to Coventry, and home.

Close to home – the cyclists approach Coventry

Joe's blog, 19th August:

Anyway, we started off on the main road, just south of Gloucester. Took a bit of time finding our way through the city, but eventually on the A38 up to Tewkesbury. Finally met up with the support crew again to stock up on snacks. We finally left the A38 in Tewkesbury – we had been on it for the last bit of Devon, through Somerset, North Somerset, Bristol, and Gloucestershire.

Up the A46, then lunch in Evesham. Wiggled up a B-road out of Evesham, then through a few villages to eventually find the Stratford

Greenway. Along into Stratford, then towards Warwick. We met up with our friend Jeremy Bevan who was joining us for a stretch on his bicycle, then a group of police officers from the Warwickshire Police Child Protection Team (colleagues of Dad's). We were finally back onto the Warwick-Coventry route, which I think I have cycled around 20 times now. The police left us just outside Warwick. I set a new top speed three times over the last leg into Coventry, and all three were going uphill. Eighteen mph, 18.5, then 19.75. We finally made it to Coventry just before 5:40.

Saturday was spent with Joe resting; me resting and checking their route north; and Helen not resting, but getting everything else organised to send Esther off to Nottingham (where she was due to start a gap year, working with a civil engineering firm), and the boys off on the next stretch.

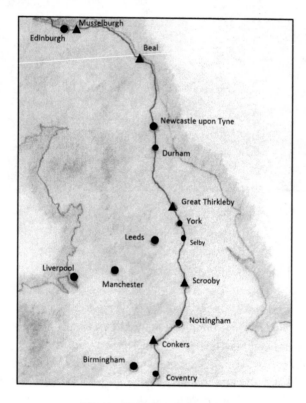

Map 4: Coventry to Edinburgh

CHAPTER 22

Letting go

From the Stuart Linnell show, BBC Coventry & Warwickshire, Sunday 21st August, to which we'd been invited to give an interview about the trip:

'David, if we can start with you, why have you all been on your bikes?'

'Well, we're doing a sponsored ride from Land's End to John O'Groats; We started last Sunday and finish in just under two weeks on Saturday the 3rd September.'

'So you're travelling through your parish at the moment.'

'Indeed. We're going to be at church this morning and hoping to have a family church cycle ride; anyone's welcome to join in; leaving at 12.30 from the steps of Holy Trinity.'

'Now, Peter, I gather you had a mishap, just one day into this.'

'I did. On the second day, we'd been pushing our bikes up a very steep hill. We got to the top and I had a mini-stroke. I ended up being admitted to Truro Hospital. So that was a bit of a blow and it's meant that I'm now out of the challenge and at home resting at the moment.'

'But recovering?'

'But recovering. I made a good, quick recovery, and I'm hoping to at least be there to see them into the finish.'

'Indeed, that would be good to do. And Joe, it's one thing to cycle this distance, but, on a unicycle? Really?'

'Yep, it's been very tiring, and it's a good challenge, but I think it's worth it; it's great fun to ride.'

'David, what are you discovering as you cycle round, as you look at this country from the benefit of the saddle of a cycle? What's occurring to you?'

'Well, lots of things actually, Stuart. I won't try and list them all, but

one of the things that occurred to me is the kindness of strangers. I mean, how many people we've met, we don't know, who've been incredibly supportive and helpful, from motorists who give us a wide berth, who slow down and don't complain, you know, who are patient with us when we sometimes get in the way; to the old lady, I think in Tiverton, when we couldn't find the start of the canal, who led us up with her walking stick to a gap in the hedge, you know. It's just really good fun, and encouraging to me to see so many good, encouraging people.'

That Sunday, I had to face the harsh reality of letting go. After all the months of preparation, putting my heart into this venture, I had to accept that I was no longer part of this cycle ride; that the most I could hope for would be to see Joe and David cross the finishing line in John O'Groats; but that, from now on, it was their ride, and I was there simply to cheer them on from the sidelines. In a sense, it always had been Joe's ride, and I was only there to support him: right from his very first dreamings, back in the autumn of 2009.

Much as I grumbled about being pushed into spending my valuable spare time in such a mad activity, I was actually quite chuffed to be doing something positive with my son. Joe, at the time, was being a fairly typical, uncommunicative teenager; and I saw this as a way of getting a bit closer to him. I think, even then, I was beginning to realise that my children's childhoods were fast whizzing past, and that they wouldn't always be around at home. So, through the months of training, including our mammoth Coventry-Bristol ride and the more recent London-Brighton, we had built up an amazing sense of shared achievement. Our communication might have still been sparse, and dominated by teenage grunts, but we had something positive to celebrate together.

Prior to the ride, I had managed to plan our route. After months of plotting it out, I felt like I owned this route, and was looking forward to cycling through some of the most stunning parts of our beautiful country: Bodmin Moor; the Meldon viaduct; cycling down the Avon Gorge, under the Clifton suspension bridge; Sherwood Forest; the Lanchester Valley railway path; the Northumbrian coast; and the Great Glen in Scotland. Not to mention the great cities of Bristol, York, Newcastle and Edinburgh.

The reality that I would not be doing so gradually sank in over the few days following my stroke. While I knew that, had I been with David and Joe, I would have adapted the route as we went along, looking for ways of making it either easier or more interesting, and responding to events as they arose; and that I would have learnt to adjust our pace, to keep us all going, without burning out; this was now no longer my gift. I had to sit back, relying on occasional text messages and updates at the end of each day, while Joe and David, on their respective cycles, worked out their own approach to cycling without me. I had to trust them to get to know each other, and to make their best decisions, without the benefit of my responsible guiding hand.

I am convinced that neither teenagers, nor sexagenarians, are responsible. I knew that they would push themselves too hard; that they wouldn't eat enough, or break for long enough; that they would lose their way and make bad decisions. And I had to accept all that. I, a middle-aged paediatrician, responsible for a mortgage, a family, and the care of my patients, was no longer responsible for this venture that had come to be so close to my heart. And I had to trust that, somehow, the enthusiasm and freedom of youth and old age would carry them through without me.

Letting go of the cycle ride wasn't the only separation I had to face that day. As Joe and David cycled north to Ashby, my daughter, Esther, also headed away from Coventry and away from home. Nineteen years ago, she had come into this world; a tiny, vulnerable baby. And I, a doting new father, had held her close, revelling in the wonder of this amazing new life. And not once imagining the pain of letting her go. I had watched her grow and mature into a beautiful and unique individual. And now, here she was, a wonderful young woman, launching out into the next stage of her life. Like all fathers, I had been dreading this moment, when my own daughter would leave home, and have to fend for herself in the big, wide world. And that, too, wasn't easy. For months I had been dwelling on this separation; reflecting back over her wonderful childhood, remembering so many little incidents – the fun times, the sad times, the struggles and the achievements. And now, all I could do was let her go, accepting

95

that Helen and I had done our best to give her a good start, trusting that the God in whom we believed would be with her, and believing that ahead of her lay a wonderful open book in which to write her own story.

So, with big hugs for both my children, and with tears in my eyes, I cheered them off that Sunday afternoon.

Letting go – saying goodbye to my family

CHAPTER 23

Cycling beyond the speed of light

Space is big. Really big. You just won't believe how vastly, hugely, mindbogglingly big it is. I mean, you may think it's a long way down the road to the chemist, but that's just peanuts to space.
- Douglas Adams, *The Hitch-Hiker's Guide to the Galaxy*

Joe and David set off from outside Holy Trinity Church, in the centre of Coventry, at 12.30 on Sunday 21st August, accompanied by a small group of cyclists from our church. They had completed the first third of their journey, and still had over 800 miles to go. Stopping for a picnic at Marston Junction, a smaller group continued, first on the Coventry canal path through Nuneaton, then on lovely roads, parallel to the Ashby canal, where they stopped for a cup of tea with our friends John and Sue Lageu on their canal boat, before heading on to the Conkers campsite at Ashby-de-la-Zouch. The next day they continued through the Midlands, passing east into Nottinghamshire, 'the Robin Hood County', which Joe decided wasn't nearly as impressive as Warwickshire's claim to be 'Shakespeare's County'. As they passed through Nottingham and into Sherwood Forest, the difficulties of doing this trip on a recumbent tricycle became very clear.

Joe's audio diary, Monday 22nd August:

Very nice roads all the way this morning; fairly hot, but not too bad on the whole. Stopped in Nottingham for a quick drink, then on through Nottingham. It's a very nice city with lots of good cycle lanes, except the one we're on at the moment (National Route 6) where David's having severe trouble getting through the gates, which are very nearly too narrow for him.

And another pair of gates. They're the type which have two thin sheets of metal sloping up and almost meeting at the top. They're just about the perfect width for me to get through, but David is having fun; in that he has to take his bag off every time, which is rather annoying when there are two gates every 100 metres or so.

But anyway, despite the gates, it's a rather nice cycle route along next to a river.

Just been brought to a slight halt by the fact that the cycle route takes us over the railway, using a bridge that has steps on either side. It's got a nice smooth ramp along the very edge of it which is designed for bikes, but essentially useless for David's tricycle. Not very helpful.

I think the conclusion we can draw from this is that the National Cycle Routes are largely not designed for tricycles. David's gone down the road a few hundred metres to see if he can find a more sensible bridge; meanwhile, I've found some rather nice blackberries, and a cat who's looking at me very suspiciously.

The cat's now wandered slightly further away but is still staring at me. David still hasn't found a bridge over and from this side of the railway it doesn't look too promising. There was clearly a bridge on the map, but I can't see any anywhere near.

Still no sign of David. I hope he finds a bridge soon or this could become slightly interesting.

Later on:

David caught up reasonably quickly and, after taking a couple of wrong turnings, due to somewhat confusingly signed cycle routes, we are, hopefully, back on the right track. Fairly nice cycle routes through some woods next to the road at the moment. Just passed a signpost, another one of the 1,000 commissioned by the Royal Bank of Scotland to mark the creation of the National Cycle Routes. I haven't seen too many of them, to be honest, which is surprising. I seem to remember there being a metal one on the Stratford Greenway, and this one here, which is significantly more colourful, but a fairly similar design. Well, we eventually made it out of Nottingham, David getting very frustrated with cycle routes. Anyway, a nice trail along a disused railway, if a bit bumpy.

It's cooled down quite a bit since earlier this morning, which is quite nice – makes it a bit more comfortable unicycling. We're not making too bad progress, although it's been rather slow over the last couple of hours. It's now 10 to four and I think we've done just over 40 miles, so we'll be lucky to make it in by seven at this rate, but that's not too bad as we're in no desperate hurry.

The trail just decided it would make it even more fun for David by being too narrow for him to fit through, but thankfully only a short bit like that. We're now back on what's just about a road, going through a rather official-looking gate into the Abbey Park, which seemed to have a guard dog by it, though it wasn't doing anything much except lying down.

We're on yet another rather bumpy section of the National Cycle Route. Had to avoid a bit and take a road earlier because it really was too narrow, and this isn't the most comfortable cycle route I've ever been on. We've just passed a rather amusing barrier, slightly below waist height saying, 'maximum height 7'2"'. Heading into Rainworth now and shortly after that we'll be going through Sherwood Forest, which, I'm hoping, will have considerably nicer trails than this one. Had a few hills now. Certainly not as flat as some the days coming into Coventry, but still very relaxed compared to Devon and Cornwall. Weather nice and cloudy, just the way we like it.

Just passed another of the Royal Bank of Scotland's National Cycle Route signs, this one a more plain iron one, though with several interesting designs carved into it going up the post. A couple of wheels, and a couple of fish skeletons for some strange reason. They are rather strange signs, most of them. Still, nice and interesting compared to the plain blue Cycle Route 6 signs; that's the word I'm looking for, interesting. Hopefully see a few more of them, cause we've only seen three out of the 1,000, if you count the one on the Stratford Greenway, and it would be nice to see a few more.

They did find more of the RBS signposts as they continued north, including one by Crask Inn in the Scottish Highlands. The Sustrans website points out that four different designs were commissioned, one from each constituent country of the UK. The fish skeletons are from the English one, designed by John Mills and entitled 'The Fossil Tree'. This abstract tree depicts the passage of time, from the earliest primitive creatures, to the ultimate demise of fossil fuel-driven technology. I, too, long for a time when we, as a global society, are less dependent on fossil fuels, and, although I may not be doing too well at the long-distance cycling, I hope soon to be back on my bike for the short commute to and from the University for my work. Meanwhile, Joe and David continued on their uni- and tricycles, Joseph definitely seeming to have the advantage on this stretch for a number of reasons, though not as far as saddle comfort goes.

Joe's audio diary, afternoon of 22nd August:

A rather amusing encounter. Riding along the cycle route, I saw a couple of walkers with dogs. One of the dogs, a very small terrier, or something similar, charged at me, barking rather loudly, ran along beside me for a bit and attempted to bite me on the foot while I was riding. It actually succeeded – not seriously but I definitely felt a bit of a nip on my foot which was quite amusing to say the least. It tried to follow me for a bit after I'd passed its owners, but obviously couldn't keep up with me. I wonder how David's going to get on with that – he's a bit closer to the level of the dog than I am.

Riding on a trail through a very large forest. I'm not entirely sure whether this is Sherwood Forest itself yet, or whether we're still just on the outskirts, but any rate, quite nice. The trail isn't actually too bad; not as nice as roads, but fairly smooth on the whole.

David's disappeared along a trail in the wrong direction because he couldn't be bothered to go through a gate, so I'll just keep eating and wait for him to get back.

Eventually got David's trike back, through a succession of gates; helped over the last two by a friendly man who obviously knew the area very well and gave us a bit of advice about the coming routes. Out of the main forest now on a much straighter route which David will no doubt be pleased about. And hopefully should stay fairly smooth all the way to Scrooby.

Oh dear, quite sore now; been riding for a rather long time with a rather large number of bumps. We decided to go along the A614 for a bit instead of continuing along the forest trails, as David and I were getting slightly tired of the bad surfaces. But it hasn't made much difference, to be honest. Well, increased the speed a lot, but my crotch is still rather sore.

They made it to the campsite at Scrooby at around 8.15, very tired and very sore, having cycled 80 miles through Nottinghamshire.

Helen, meanwhile, having set up the campsite, had managed to double back to Nottingham to see Esther settled into her temporary accommodation, and started in her 'year in industry' placement. The next day, rather disillusioned with off-road cycle paths, Joe and David followed a long stretch of the A19 through Doncaster to Selby.

It was along this section that Joe's handlebar snapped. The gruelling routine of Land's End to John O'Groats had taken its toll – this time on the handlebar bracket. Long distance unicycles have a short handlebar sticking forward from the seat. This allows the rider to grip with their hands, helping a bit with balance, and taking some of the pressure off the legs. It also hosts a brake – useful for going downhill, where, with a little bit of gentle pressure, just enough friction is generated to slow down the descent, without throwing the cyclist violently forward off the saddle. As they were cycling along the A19, Joe found his handlebars starting to come loose: the bracket attaching them to the seat had snapped.

Joe's blog, 23rd August:

I continued riding (not much choice at that stage), and we made it into Selby after a somewhat nerve-wracking 10 miles.

In Selby, they scouted around for somewhere to get it fixed:

After finding helpful people in two bike shops and a garage, we were eventually directed to an engineering shop on the other side of town, which should be able to weld the bracket. After riding across Selby with my handlebars on my lap (they were still attached to the wheel by the brake cable), we discovered that the place was closed for the week. Detaching the brake cable, we continued up towards York, slowly and – for me – painfully.

Meanwhile, Helen, in the support car, had managed to get hold of Roger at Unicycle.com. Once again, being not too far from the makers, she managed to do a diversion up to Stockton, pick up a new bracket (and a spare for the other side – predictably, having taken a greater strain, that one finally gave way up in Scotland), and drive back to meet Joe and David on the far side of York. Joe had cycled an incredible 25 miles on his unicycle, holding his handlebars as he went. Not an experience he was keen to repeat. This was compensated for a bit by their discovery of a delightful, and smooth, cycle path into York itself – the Solar System Cycle Way.

Joe's audio diary, 23rd August:

Very impressed with the Selby to York cycle route, it's definitely the nicest one we've been on for quite a while. Just passed another Royal Bank of Scotland signpost, our fourth one of the trip so far. This one a fairly plain black one. I didn't get too much of a chance to look at it. Yep, as I said, a fairly nice cycle route and Oh! Oh, Oh, Oh! David, this is Pluto! And yes, this is the Solar System route. We have just found Pluto. Let's see. A scale model of the Solar System, a little over 10k. A single stride will take you over 500,000 km; brisk walking speed will take you at over three times the speed of light. So, according to this, David and I will easily be travelling at 10 times the speed of light along this route, which will make a change from our slow progress through the hills of Devon and Cornwall. We're just outside Pluto now and Neptune is another 1,413,100,000 km, otherwise known as about 2.5k.

According to this scale, the centre of the Milky Way is 300 million miles away, which is quite an impressive distance, and the most distant objects observed in the Universe are 27 billion light years away, so far away that you shouldn't even think of cycling there. Then again, some people would say that about Land's End to John O'Groats.

Of course, the fact that we're travelling at 10 times the speed of light also makes me rather nervous, due to the fact that, with the loss of the handlebars, I've also lost my brake.

Some rather interesting benches with a series of tunnel-like structures behind them, but sadly no sign of either Neptune or David. Perhaps David's died due to the lack of oxygen in outer space.

I wonder if it's possible to cycle when there's no gravity?

And I've reached Neptune. It's rather more impressive than Pluto; it's got a bit of information about the planet and stuff, rather than the bus-shelter type of structure which was all we could see at the last point. It may interest you to know that it's actually 200 million km further from Neptune to

Uranus than it is from Pluto to Neptune. Rather strange; I'd always assumed that planets get closer together, which they do, but obviously not in this particular case. Anyway, going to press on again. It's 2.8 km to Uranus.

Did I say 2.8 km? I'm sorry, I obviously meant 1,629,600,000.

We've now reached Uranus, obviously the third planet in the direction we're going. I won't bore you with all the details, but the sign says it was the first planet to be discovered in modern times. The date: March 13th 1781. The distance from here to Saturn is fairly similar to the distance between Neptune and Pluto. If the information is correct, which I think it is, then we're now around half-way through the Solar System. Which means the planets are going to have to get significantly closer together after Saturn. Anyway, onwards, hopefully, if I'm not too sore.

Just passed a rather large model of a NASA satellite, several times bigger than all the planets we've seen so far. We're now at Saturn, which is quite a bit bigger than Uranus and Neptune. Obviously, second in size to Jupiter. It's roughly 650 million km to Jupiter, so the distances are getting shorter now.

Just passed a rather impressive sculpture of a man fishing on top of a bridge, accompanied by his dog and his bicycle. Very large, made out of some kind of metal poles. Obviously nothing to do with the Solar System, but still adds to the general feel of the route.

Now at Jupiter, with 550 million km to go to Mars.

Another Royal Bank of Scotland signpost, this one a blue post, with red and yellow arrows at the top. And we're randomly going through a series of houses in the middle of the Solar System.

We've now arrived at the model of Mars. This one obviously significantly smaller than the gas giants we've been seeing. It's about the width of my little finger; Neptune and Uranus were, I think, around the size of my wrist; Jupiter and Saturn obviously even bigger than that. So, Mars is significantly smaller. Nice to know they're keeping the models to scale. And only 78 million km to earth; getting very short now.

Earth and the moon, looking something like 70 cm apart. Earth is about the width of two fingers, meaning Land's End to John O'Groats is probably something in the region of 2 mm on this model, possibly even less than that – not really very much of a challenge. Now, I'm fairly certain that it's about eight light minutes from earth to the sun, so, theoretically, I should be able to make it to the sun in less than a minute. I think I might just test that theory out.

Earth to the Sun, precisely 42 seconds. And I imagine I could have done it even quicker if I'd had handlebars. David seems to have been held up somewhere between Venus and Mercury; so he might have to go back and retime himself. Anyway, while I'm waiting for him, the diameter of the Sun is 1.4 million kilometres. It rotates once every 25.4 days, and it contains 99.8% of the mass of the Solar System, which is rather impressive. I see the model of it just above me here, looking very large; from here it looks like the width is somewhere between one and a half to two times the wheel of my unicycle.

Joe retraced his steps a bit to look at Venus and Mercury, just 87 metres (or 50 million km) apart, before leaving the Solar system and heading on to York.

An unusual convoy – David and Joe are joined by Roger on another unicycle

The next day turned out to be one of the most gruelling of the whole trip. Having been joined in North Allerton by Roger, who runs Unicycle.com, on his unicycle, they made good progress all the way to Durham, covering 50 miles in just five and a half hours. Joe was enjoying the day's riding, in near-perfect riding conditions, and was optimistic about making it to Newcastle somewhere between 6.30 and 7.00. It was around this point that things started to go wrong. Joe got stung by a wasp around five miles before Durham, which wasn't too much fun. David's chain got jammed, though thankfully Roger was still around to fix it. Then Roger left, and Joe and David rode out of Durham along the wrong cycle path. Ten miles later, after riding along a rather poor cycle path, Joe stopped to wait for David, who wasn't having much fun riding uphill on that surface. It was then they realised they were in completely the wrong place. After 10 more miles up and down several hills, into a headwind, they were just south of where the cycle path should have taken them, with two more very steep hills ahead of them.

We started off well; we were making great time;
We'd be finished by six; it was all going fine.
Then we got into Durham and things began to go wrong.
We took a wrong turn; we went left, not straight on.
Then 10 miles of riding up a steep, rocky hill;
David took ages and I took a chill.
Then we looked at the map, and at last we could see:
We were 10 miles south of where we should be.

So we rode through the wind, and we rode through the rain;
We rode over the hills, we rode on, through the pain.
We began to get tired, we began to get sore.
We kept riding on, for two hours, or more.
But we finally made it, only three hours late.
We'd done it, we'd finished, at one hour past eight.

CHAPTER 24

Sweeping the country

We were now in David's home territory. As Joe cycled into Newcastle and took advantage of a hot bath and plenty of good food, David had cycled on into the night, taking yet another wrong turning, but eventually arriving with friends at Angerton, near Morpeth, shortly before midnight. I, having had a week recuperating at home, had hitched a lift with Elizabeth, along with Neo, to join Helen and Joe in Newcastle with our university friends, Justin and Mary.

Newcastle, as we found, is a wonderful city, and the inhabitants seemed friendly and welcoming. All, that is, apart from one of Justin and Mary's neighbours: a Geordie cat, who did not take well to Neo trying to play with it shortly after we arrived. Neo definitely came off the worse from that encounter. With a loud screech, followed by a whimper, Neo came running out of the encounter, with his tail between his legs, and a torn ear. We bundled him into Justin and Mary's house, where he proceeded to violently shake his head, covering the hallway in a spattering of blood. Their house looked as though a massacre had just taken place. Twenty minutes of firm pressure on the ear did not stem the flow and Neo ended up having stitches under anaesthetic, and had to suffer the humiliation of a purple head bandage and a 'collar of shame'.

After a well-earned rest day for the two cyclists, they set off from their respective starting points early on the Friday, meeting up in Morpeth for a great send-off by a number of friends. David had spent fourteen years as vicar in nearby Mitford before moving to Holy Trinity, Coventry. He and Elizabeth had obviously found a great home there, welcomed by the community, and establishing some long-lasting friendships. Two of their friends, Wendy and John, joined David and Joe for the day's ride, as did Jane Hutton, a friend of ours from Coventry, who took a couple of days out of a northern cycling tour to join the team. Once again, the camaraderie provided by friends gave a welcome boost to the intrepid cyclists and to the team as a whole. It also gave a little diversion for Helen and me, as Jane, a professor of statistics, with an eye for beauty, had spotted a very nice piece of blue glass in a studio window in Warkworth, and commissioned us to go back and buy it for her. Joe, somehow didn't appear to appreciate the value of fine art.

The invalids – Peter and Neo recuperating

Joe's audio diary, 26th August:

Very amusing. Just met up with Mum and Dad, and Neo who's now got his bandage back on. Jane's been discussing with them whether she wants to buy a piece of glass that she saw in a gallery in the last town. She's going to send them back to get it, 'cause she didn't quite have time while we were there, but she's just stopping to check a gallery here as well, to see if they've got anything she'd like even more. David's gone shooting off ahead somewhere, so I'm slowly making my way up the hill somewhere between David and Jane. All very silly, but good fun.

With me out of the running, the nature of the ride, I think, changed. Neither David nor Joe were good at keeping in touch, and Helen, as the support team, was often left wondering where they were and how they were getting on. Meanwhile, the two of them rode on, in their very different styles: Joe keeping up a steady eight to 12 miles per hour, while David crawled up each hill at a much more sedate pace, before whizzing down the other side at breakneck speeds. Inevitably, it seemed that they spent large parts of each day riding in splendid isolation, and often Joe would spend long periods waiting at the top of a hill for David to catch up. When they got to downhill stretches, David would, in his turn, speed ahead, revelling in the freedom, singing loud hymns of praise, and enjoying the opportunities to think and reflect; then spending long periods waiting for Joe to rejoin him at the bottom.

And yet, in spite of Helen's and my misgivings, it seemed to work. The combination of David's sexagenarian enthusiasm and Joe's teenage determination seemed to carry them through. And they worked together, in their own way, as a team; each looking out for the other, regrouping from time to time, debating and agreeing the routes and any diversions, and enjoying an unusual but deep bond: two very different characters, from different generations, joined together in a mutual challenge.

For Joe, this journey was perhaps primarily about achieving something few had achieved; a new challenge for him, an opportunity to do something worthwhile in raising money for charity, and a chance to discover more about himself and to see something more of our wonderful country. For David, it was all that, but also, perhaps, an opportunity to express something of what he believed in.

A week before we set off on our cycle ride, England was racked by riots and looting. Starting in Tottenham, sparked by the police shooting of 29-year-old Mark Duggan, the riots spread to other parts of the city and across the country. Thousands took to the streets over the ensuing nights, attacking police, looting shops, and damaging property. In Birmingham, three young Asian men were killed while trying to defend their property from looters. The father of one of them, Tariq Jahan, spoke out powerfully afterwards with a message of reconciliation: 'The three sacrificed their lives. It took their lives for the nation to calm down and realise that, you know, it's not necessary. And I'm grateful to the young youth that listened and did calm down. And I'm very grateful to the Muslim community for not taking it any further.'

Just before interviewing us on BBC Coventry and Warwickshire on the 21st August, Stuart Linnell reported on the impact of that one man: 'If there is a lasting image or memory that should come from what happened a couple of weeks ago, it shouldn't be the burning down of the furniture store in Tottenham, it shouldn't be people taking flat screen televisions out of shops, it should be the dignity of Tariq Jahan.' We were all deeply affected by that report, and by the love and commitment of the two Muslim fathers and sons who were interviewed before us about Ramadan.

The riots and looting were disturbing events, revealing some of the turmoil, disillusionment and despair that seems so prevalent in our country, but also the greed and selfishness that pervades all levels of our society: not just the looters, flagrantly disregarding the law, and showing no respect for others' property; but also the bankers, politicians, media tycoons and others, who seem equally liable to flaunt or bend the rules for their own gain, and who are, perhaps, far more to blame than any young hoodie. I guess the truth is, at heart, that each of us is selfish: am I, with my secure job, my comfortable doctor's salary and my nice home, really any better than a fat-cat banker, drawing an obscene salary plus bonuses, or than a deprived, unemployed young man, struggling to make ends meet for his family, who takes advantage of a breakdown in law and order to try and get something nice for his children?

But alongside those negative images of our contemporary society, there was also a powerful message of hope. The morning after the riots, more people took to the streets in Clapham, Hackney and elsewhere; armed this time, not with bricks and bottles, but with brooms. The simple broom became a symbol of hope and a fresh start. David picked up on this mood of hope, and cycled across our nation with a broom sticking up behind him, strapped to his tricycle, praying this prayer of hope as he went:

Sweep away, O Lord,
all pride and bitterness,
all greed and despair
from my heart,
and from the heart of our country.

Help us to work with all those who seek
your justice and compassion,
your kindness and peace;
that all may flourish
through the gracious power of Jesus Christ,
Servant and Saviour of all.

CHAPTER 25

Coasts, castles and calories

Originally launched in 1918 as Bassett's Peace Babies, to celebrate the end of the First World War, everyone will enjoy eating these delicious treats. You can have fun choosing from the different flavoured soft jelly sweets, then enjoy eating the baby shapes. Will it be head first? And they taste great, because they are made only with natural colours and natural flavours, so what are you waiting for?

From Bassett's Jelly Babies

One of the biggest challenges faced by long-distance cyclists seems to be getting enough food. This is even more so for a long-distance unicyclist, as the constant pedalling, coupled with the effort involved in balancing, chews up calories at a phenomenal rate. These need to be replaced, but with care: large sugar doses, such as Mars bars, are great at giving a rapid boost to energy, but this quickly wears off; so more slow-release carbohydrates are also required. At the same time, consuming large amounts of stodgy food just before cycling doesn't work well, as the food sits in your stomach, digesting poorly, and potentially giving you cramps. Judging by the comments of others, Helen worked out that Joe would need something between 4,000 and 6,000 calories a day. Joe started on this in the run-up to the ride:

Breakfast – A large bowl of cereal, a 'Frijj' milkshake, a yoghurt.
Lunch – Another yoghurt, a cereal bar, a smoothie, a steak slice, a Cornish pastie.
Tea – Pasta. Another 'Frijj'.
Supper – Half a pizza. A slice of syrup cake. Anything else I can bring myself to eat – today, two fried eggs and a Mars bar.

A hot chocolate.

However, all that is apparently not quite enough. So from today, I've started on protein shakes, from a sports nutrition shop in Coventry. From now until the end of the ride, I'll be having two or three a day. They're fairly nice – rather like cold hot chocolate, though I'm sure I'll be sick of them by the end of the ride. Obviously, during the ride I introduce energy drinks, more chocolate, and anything else I can eat.

Keeping it going wasn't so easy. Joe somehow didn't really seem to appreciate all the sandwiches, bananas, snacks, energy drinks and other calories Helen loaded him down with; and with me out of the running, he had to carry all this in a small backpack, rather than my panniers. Neither Joe nor David seemed to be particularly good at stopping for proper food breaks, and it seemed that Joe would often snatch a few bites at a time while waiting for David to catch up after uphill stretches. Perhaps, though, that worked out quite well as a regular, small intake of energy. On some days it seemed to take Joe several attempts to finish just one sandwich:

Mmmm. Squashed sandwiches with processed cheese. Don't we love it? I'm having a rather late lunch in the middle of what may or may not be Sherwood Forest; David's disappeared along a trail in the wrong direction because he couldn't be bothered to go through a gate, so I'll just keep eating and wait for him to get back.

On another day, at Embleton, in Northumberland:

David and Jane caught us up. After David had stopped to check his phone, I overtook him, but, as I said, both of them caught us up. I failed to finish my cheese sandwich for, I think, the third time now [I think a different cheese sandwich from the one in Sherwood Forest]. *I've been getting a few bites of it every time we stop and now I'm about three quarters of the way through it. Sadly, I can't really say it's been worth the wait – it's only processed cheese. Oh well, it's good energy or something like that. I might finish it at the next break if I'm lucky.*

In contrast to the processed cheese sandwiches, Joe seemed to get on far better with Jelly Babies:

We had made very good progress, with David and Jane riding very fast, and I, powered forward by Jelly Babies. After a recommendation by Justin, the support crew had bought a large packet. A slight misunderstanding saw me consuming half over the day, rather than just a few, so I ended up getting around 1,000 calories from Jelly Babies today! Still, it means I had the energy.

The Jelly Babies certainly kept him going well, and the two of them, accompanied by Jane, Wendy and John, stormed up the Northumberland coast. They were now cycling through some of the most magnificent scenery this country has to offer, though the appreciation of this dawned rather slowly on Joe. Joe did the first 13-mile section to Morpeth on his own, including one short stretch on a busy section of the A1. In Morpeth, he joined up with the others and the newly-revived team headed north through Ulgham (for some reason pronounced Uffham), to join the coast at Amble. Amble claims the title of 'the Friendliest Port', which apparently stems from the 1930s, when *RMS Mauretania* was steaming up the British coast on her final voyage to a breaker's yard at Rosyth. The Amble Town Council sent a telegram to the ship saying, 'still the finest ship on the seas', to which the *Mauretania* replied with greetings 'to the last and friendliest port in England'. Joe describes their route along the coastal cycle path; from his audio diary, 26th August:

On the route from Morpeth to Warkworth at the moment. We're obviously now going along the Northumberland coast, which is another area of outstanding natural beauty. It's not actually looking that incredible at the moment, but I'm sure it will get better later.

Just stopping for a break in a very nice coffee shop in Warkworth. About 13 miles covered so far; it's been a very nice day of riding. The rain hasn't started yet, so it's been fairly good weather and we're making pretty good time on the whole.

Now getting some very nice views of the sea – essentially the first time since the first couple of days in Cornwall. Still rather a long way to go until we get to the sea in the North of Scotland, but it is nice to be back by the coast for a bit at any rate.

Now cycling along right next to the beach. You can very clearly smell the sea now, which is rather nice, as well as being able to see it, obviously. I've just been passed by a rescue helicopter going somewhere or other. I think I may have seen it flying in the opposite direction earlier, so it may have just picked someone up.

Rather bumpy route along right next to the sea. It's actually the closest we've been to it at any point on the journey I think, even at Land's End. Yup, rather bumpy.

National Cycle Route 1. Proving to be rather too sandy and narrow for David's tricycle, and, to be honest, it really is far more like a footpath than a cycle route along here. I'm not having too much fun but, ignoring the quality of the route, it's very nice scenery, up towards Dunstanburgh Castle. My wheel has now touched the sea, both in Cornwall and in Northumberland. And will hopefully touch it again at John O'Groats.

Walking is proving to be more comfortable than cycling for several sections of the route. I think David, going back on the road, had the right idea. He's probably going about five times as fast as us at the moment, and will almost certainly make it to the end of this section of the route well before we do. I'm really hoping the cycle track's going to improve fairly soon, 'cause I'm getting slightly bored of walking, but there's not a huge amount I can do about it. Still lovely scenery, though, again, I would have preferred the road.

Jane just got stuck in a rut and rather spectacularly crashed over onto one side.

Everything going very crazy. We've just met up with one of David's friends called John, who will be joining us when we get to Embleton; he's just driving up there. Jane's gone off to do a bit more of the coastal route, I've opted to stick on the road, and David is still on another bit of road, coming up towards Embleton. So hopefully we should all meet up in Embleton in a couple of miles, but it could potentially go a bit haywire. Anyway, I'm sure Jane's getting very nice scenery around there, but I've opted to stay on the road.

I can see Dunstanburgh Castle over off to our right (I sounded like a tour guide there), with a few rather large dunes in the area, which I'm sure Jane will have fun cycling over.

Finally met up with everyone in one of the pubs in Embleton. It's now 25 past three and we've got just under 30 miles left to go. John is intending to join us for around an hour. We're just discussing speeds on David's trike – a fairly common topic of conversation.

Just having a brief stop in Bamburgh, up the road a bit from a rather impressive castle. We've made very good progress, around 55 miles in between four and a half and five and a half hours, depending on whether you're me or David; should hopefully finish fairly soon. We said goodbye to John and Wendy just outside Seahouses. And so now it's just the three of us.

David, Joe and Jane arrived at Beal at around half past six; one of their earliest finishes. The Barn at Beal was one of the nicest campsites of the whole trip, with just a few pitches, up on a ridge, looking out over Holy Island to the North Sea. The weather was perfect, and after a quick cup of tea, Joe, Jane, Helen and I drove over the causeway to Holy Island, where we wandered peacefully around the south end, enjoying the stillness of the church and priory grounds. This was another of those places at which I would have loved to linger, soaking up the deep-rooted spirituality of the island. Once again, though, that will have to wait for another, more leisurely time.

The Barn at Beal – David and Joe set off, accompanied by Jane

The next day, David, Joe and Jane set off again, through Berwick, where David, once more, stopped to get some repairs done to his tricycle gears. Jane and Joe decided to press on, up the A1, assuming that David would have no trouble catching them up.

Joe's Blog, 27th August:

We crossed the border into Scotland just after half 12, with David still getting the trike fixed in England. Nothing spectacular about the border, but it still gave a very nice sense of progress. At around that point, we also passed two thirds of the way. I now feel a very definite sense of pride in saying that we've come from Land's End; in Cornwall, it was always 'Oh, you haven't come far, then!'

On up the A1, with some very nice scenery along the coast. We made very good progress over the rest of the day, with David (gears now permanently fixed) catching us up about 20 miles past the border.

The team reached the campsite in Musselburgh at about 10 past six, just seconds before a very heavy shower of rain. Jane, having spent two inspiring and energetic days with the lads, waited for the shower to pass and carried on into Edinburgh (getting caught almost immediately in a second, equally heavy, downpour) to stay with a friend. The following morning, David and Joe themselves pushed on into Edinburgh, to start their final 400-mile stretch of the journey, in style, joining friends Pam and Jean for a coffee/hot chocolate at Starbucks on Prince's Street.

As Joe, David and Jane pedalled on to Edinburgh, and Helen and I covered the same route in the car, Elizabeth, sadly, had to leave us all to head south to be with her mother, Peggy, who was seriously ill in hospital. Peggy had suffered a stroke a month previously, and, unlike me, this had been a full-blown stroke, from which she did not recover. Three days later, as David and Joe cycled up the Great Glen in Scotland, Peggy died peacefully in her hospital bed. She had lived a full and long life (into her nineties), and had remained active right up to her stroke – she had managed to get to David's birthday party the previous month, and all her family had been able to see her in the last days. For Elizabeth and David, these memories of a full life were clearly mixed with the grief of losing someone close. For all of us, it seemed somehow that Elizabeth's and Peggy's story was a part of ours too, and that the whole of life – health, illness, grief and loss – was reflected over these three weeks, in a small way, in our little family. All that was missing, perhaps, was birth and marriage, but we were in no rush to try and incorporate those into the next few days.

Two windswept cyclists warm up in Starbucks

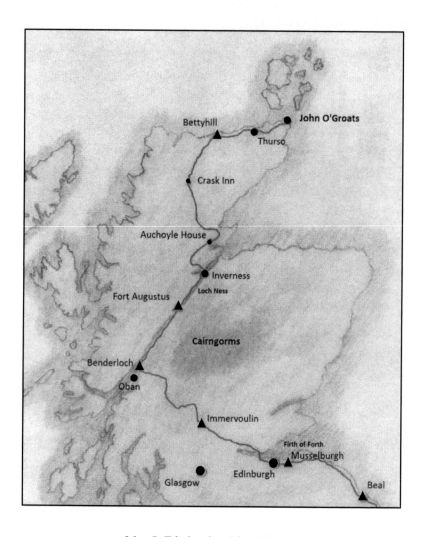

Map 5: Edinburgh to John O'Groats

CHAPTER 26

Nice place, Scotland

Having made it to Scotland, Joe and David seemed to find a new lease of energy, as they covered some of the most awe-inspiring scenery our islands have to offer. This was Joe's first taste of Scotland, and he loved it. After a week of steady cycling through the flat plains of England, the lads were feeling fit and energetic, and the Scottish climbs, though higher than those of Cornwall, seemed somehow less steep and more manageable. More of a challenge, at least on their first day through Edinburgh and up the Forth valley, was the strong head wind, as Joe explained:

The idea behind riding Land's End to John O'Groats, rather than vice versa, was to get the prevailing wind behind us. All very sensible, in theory. However, the route we've taken means that we've been riding west for the last couple of days. Today, this meant riding straight into the wind. A very strong wind, for that matter.

Coming into Edinburgh, they skirted round Arthur's Seat, and Joe, correctly, anticipated my reaction when I heard his dictation describing it as 'a large, rocky hill':

Rather a large rocky hill just over to my right now. Thankfully we're going round it rather than over it. I'm sure that when Dad's typing this up, he will put some sort of a mention as to what that is.

Joe also had fun with reinterpreting the name of their route into the city:

Now riding along the Innocent Cycle Path through Edinburgh; it used to be the Innocent railway. It would be very amusing if you said it with a proper Coventry accent: it would be a bit of an innocent psycho-path. Going through Edinburgh at the moment, into a rather strong headwind. It's not quite as bad along here as it was on the road, but still not making riding much fun. We're now going into a rather long tunnel. I'll see if I can get a bit of an echo later on. Headwind a little better inside the tunnel thankfully; it has been making rather slow riding so far. We're now out of the tunnel and through a series of houses. Yeah, not through the houses themselves, just along a rather small path next to them. Anyway, heading towards the city centre, about half an hour later than we were expecting, but never mind.

On the far side of Edinburgh, Helen and I met David and Joe at the viewpoint on the near side of the Forth road bridge. A large sign warned motorists of high winds, and they certainly were. Joe, in particular, had to lean quite hard to the left as he crossed the bridge.

High winds indeed!

Joe's audio diary, 28th August:

Now riding over the Forth Bridge. Rather large, rather windy, quite a lot of boats over to my left, and impressive views to be honest, as I get towards the top of it. Also, the landscape looks fairly flat on the other side from here, so we might get a bit of reasonably easy riding for a bit, which would be nice.

Half-way across now. It's really, really windy; I'm just permanently leaning into the wind… Hopefully will have a bit more shelter when we come off the bridge.

Finally over the bridge and into the Kingdom of Fife.

Once over the bridge, they had a good ride up past Stirling to Callander and then into the first stretches of the Trossachs. The wind stayed against them for most of the day, although fortunately they seemed to miss the heavy downpours that swept through Edinburgh later that day.

Joe's audio diary:

Fairly long hill coming up out of Inverkeithing. Just waiting for David, who, I imagine, will be a few minutes longer. Yeah. Not actually too bad – I started off very slowly on the hill, but then a lot easier from then onwards. The wind's definitely a bit easier now. And David's just coming over the top now, well done him. It's 20 to two, so not one of our fastest days, but we're not doing too badly now.

Later that day:

Just passed Stirling and heading onwards towards the Bridge of Allan and then up north towards the campsite. It's quarter to six and we've got somewhere in the region of 15 miles left. Just stopped because I can see the Wallace monument on ahead to my right, looking rather impressive. We're skirting round the hill, which is very nice, and we've had a flat route for quite a while. The headwind came back rather strongly a few miles ago, but it's not too bad at the moment. So, hopefully, make it to the campsite in reasonable time.

About 10 miles left to go now. Just stopped for a quick break and put my unicycle down on the grass. And since then I've had two cars, two drivers rather, give me a thumbs up, which is strange, 'cause they can't have seen the unicycle, and they can't have seen me before, 'cause they've come from behind me, so I'm not entirely sure why that was, but still encouraging, so it's all good. I should probably go and catch up with David now.

In Callander now. It's just about half-seven, and David's decided to go shopping in one of two outdoors stores, both of which have closing down sales, and are about 50 metres from each other, possibly even less.

Later still:

Yep, we're still riding. The route's turned out to be longer than it should have been, again. And I'm absolutely exhausted. Made slightly better by the fact that we've got a very nice view of the sunset over the loch [Loch Lubnaig]. Had some fairly friendly motorists actually, a few giving me thumbs up as they passed, and also one guy, a while back, who's obviously a professional photographer, stopped at three points down the road to take pictures of me and David, which was rather nice. Yeah, the sunset's very nice. Just a shame we're still riding, rather than sitting in the campsite watching it.

Joe's Blog, 28th August:

We eventually made it in around half-eight. Met up with grandparents, who are camping with us for some length of time unknown to me. More than 850 miles covered – if we were doing a normal length route, we'd practically be there now.

The next day started with a long ride up from Strathyre, past the Kingshouse Hotel and Lochearnhead to the Glenogle Pass at 288 metres: the second highest point on their journey (they managed to top 300 metres on Bodmin Moor). Once again, the scenery was stunning, and topped by an excellent lunch break – well worth the stop.

Joe's Blog, 29th August:

Uphill for a fairly long stretch this morning, but still made it to the lunch break in very good time – beating the support team by about 15 minutes. Lunch was at The Real Food Café in Tyndrum. Recommended to us by Paul as the best fish and chip shop in Scotland, we thought we should probably try it. Another Lejog unicyclist had stopped there a few years ago, but they were still so impressed by the challenge that David and I got a free drink! Very nice fish and chips, rounded off by a mammoth six person pudding – the 'West Highland Way Hey Hey': a kind of chocolate trifle, with large amounts of cream, chocolate, marshmallows, sponge, fruit and custard, it seemed to fuel us on the way for the next 35 miles!

From Tyndrum, it was wonderful gentle riding for them, down the magnificent Glen Lochy to the Strath of Orchy and Loch Awe.

Joe's audio diary:

Very nice riding at the moment, along next to a river, still hills and forest on pretty much every side, but the river definitely adding to it a bit; obviously flat as well, which is very nice. A few ups and downs, but we're making good progress.

Met up with Paul, and also Alick, who will be riding with us for six miles or so, before Anna takes over. Somewhere in the region of 10 miles to the campsite now. Rather hilly, so I've left David and the others a bit of a way behind; I'm sure they'll catch up when we start going back down towards the coast. Making very good progress. At the rate we're going, we'll have done 35 miles in probably less than three and a half hours by the time we make it to the campsite, which is pretty good on the whole.

Only four days left! It's already starting to feel like we're nearly there. And it's been great fun, but I will certainly be glad to finish.

We camped that night by the sea at Benderloch, and Neo, unconstrained by bandages, leads, or our fear of passing sheep, enjoyed racing up and down the sand. David and Joe had been joined for bits of these two days by friends of ours from Coventry who were on holiday in the area. Over the next two days, Joe and

David cycled over 100 miles up the Great Glen – an incredible geological fault line that cuts Scotland in two, providing a passage from the southwest to the northeast coasts of Scotland, and flanked by some of Scotland's finest mountains, including, of course, Ben Nevis.

Joe's Blog, 30th August:

The most obvious thing to say about today is that it was one of the most enjoyable days of riding I've had for a long time. It began with an incredible cycle route up towards Fort William – smooth tarmac all the way, brilliant views over the loch, etc. Even a slight tailwind, making a very nice change from the headwinds of the last few days. This was only spoiled slightly by David getting the first puncture of the ride, after 950 miles of riding. That was fixed soon enough, then we headed on along the road towards the fort.

We had lunch at a small picnic area next to the second loch of the day. Again, amazing views over the loch. At this point, Alick joined us for the stretch into Fort William. Paul had been with us from the start of the day, providing great company, along with some useful local knowledge. Along the main road into Fort William, then along a cycle route on to the canal. We left David at a bike shop, and he proceeded to take a different route for the next 15 miles.

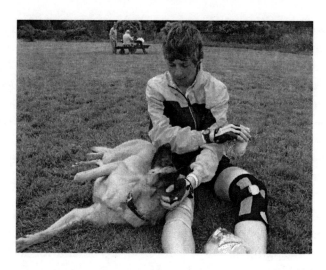

Joe and Neo enjoy a lunch break together

Joe's audio diary, that day:

Now waiting at the bottom of Neptune's Staircase, about to do a stretch along the canal. Forty-three miles covered now. Very impressive-looking peaks we can see from over here, the central one, Ben Nevis, with the top completely covered in cloud, so I can't really see how high it actually is, and quite a few others around it, also going up into the clouds. All fairly impressive, to be perfectly honest. Nice place, Scotland.

Now a sense of anticipation as we wait for the steam engine to arrive, which we can hear in the distance, and hopefully it will come into sight soon and cross over the bridge and, oh yes, there it is. That's very impressive, it's also going backwards, interesting. Yes, a very smart black engine, going backwards and several carriages being towed in front of it. Oh yes! Very smart. Lots of people waving out of the window, very nice. I'm still not entirely sure why it's going backwards, but oh well.

[This was the Jacobite Express, made famous as the Hogwarts Express, which travels from Fort William to Mallaig, crossing the amazing Glenfinnan viaduct overlooking Loch Shiel.]

Cycling along the canal towpath now. Neptune's Staircase, obviously a flight of locks, is actually very short, only about four locks altogether [In fact eight locks in total, and the longest staircase in Britain!]. *Impressively wide canal, looks around three times the width of the normal ones in England. Going slowly along here, but still not too bad. David's gone round the road so will probably be waiting for us at the end.*

A bit later:

We've left the canal now, just waiting for Paul and Anna at the top of a fairly large hill. I think it's the steepest we've had in Scotland – a nice challenge, not too difficult compared to anything in Cornwall and Devon. Nice views from the top – actually, very nice, river below us and then, yeah, the whole valley of the river before you get to the mountains on the other side – it's pretty nice. The nice thing about the hill is that it gave me a sense of how much I've improved during the ride, because I really think that, before I started, I would have really struggled up that. But I basically shot straight up it without even feeling particularly tired. I imagine it's going to take the cyclists a bit longer though. Still, it gives me a nice break, so I'm not complaining. There's a Commando monument somewhere around here where hopefully we'll be meeting up with David, if he hasn't got bored of waiting and gone on.

Joe's Blog, that evening:

We met up with David again, and left the Doggetts. It's been great to have them with us here in Scotland. David and I then rode on towards Fort Augustus. Very long downhill stretch towards the loch (very good for David), during which the sun came out for the first time in about four days. Shortly after this, we met a German cyclist who has cycled 2600 km from Germany over the last three weeks. Into the campsite just after seven, after a very enjoyable 75 miles.

The following day Joe and David rode all the way up beside Loch Ness to Inverness where Helen and I, after struggling with the traffic and trying to find a place to park a car and trailer, joined them for a brief lunch break in the shadow of Inverness Castle, and a statue of Faith, Hope and Charity.

Joe's Blog, 31st August:

A rather late start, but we made good progress riding along Loch Ness. A bit hilly, but a slight tailwind kept our speed up. No sign of the monster...

We stopped for lunch in Inverness, next to the river. A fairly strong current was carrying a few seagulls down the river, prompting David to come out with the amazing comment: 'If that seagull had gears, I'd be telling it to watch out, because it's going backwards!'

Loch Ness – a picture of calm

CHAPTER 27

And the paediatrician

Refuah Shelema, Refuas HaNefesh U'Refuas HaGuf:
A Hebrew blessing, sent by a paediatric colleague of mine; wishing complete healing of spirit and body.

As Joe and David continued their journey, pedalling on through the wilds of Scotland, I too continued on my, very different, journey. Although my position was very different, and not what I had anticipated, it seemed to me that this wasn't, in fact, a new journey, but rather a continuation of an ongoing journey; one that had started long before. I had only once before been on the receiving end of hospital-based health care: as an 11-year-old schoolboy with appendicitis, in Hong Kong, where I had spent the first 19 years of my life. I shared a two-bedded room with an elderly Chinese gentleman who'd had his gall bladder removed, and spoke very little English. I, to my eternal shame, spoke even less Cantonese, so our communication consisted of smiles and gestures. I spent the best part of the Easter holidays in that hospital room, which, while frustrating, did have the slight mitigating benefit of winning me plenty of chocolate Easter eggs from the nurses who doted on me, and from the gentleman's family, to whom I was an object of great interest and concern. Of more interest to me, however, was the offending organ, which I kept for a long time afterwards in a little bottle of formalin, showing it off as my trophy to anyone who cared to have a look. I seem to remember one end of the said appendix was neatly clamped, like the end of a tube of toothpaste; while the other was ragged and mangy, suggesting that it had, in fact, perforated, and that, presumably, I had been really quite unwell at the time.

My fascination with this little part of me did not attract me to the wonders of a career in pathology (it was only recently, with my growing involvement in SIDS research and clinical care, that I have come to properly respect and understand the valuable role played by pathologists, and their bizarre fascination with incomprehensible pink and purple slides). The experience was nevertheless a turning point for me and the origin of my journey into the wonderful world of medicine. Having endured (and even enjoyed) the rigours of medical school and house jobs, and the seemingly never-ending cycle of nights on call, nights recovering from being on call, and nights spent revising for my membership exams, I finally got to the stage where I could call myself a paediatrician. I loved every aspect of my work, and particularly the clinical contact with children and parents.

In the early years of my training, there were two aspects of paediatrics (excluding pathology and biochemistry, neither of which I could understand), which really didn't appeal to me, and which I was convinced I would not pursue: academic research, and child protection practice. So, it is with some amusement that I find myself now, 14 years into my consultant career, as an academic paediatrician with special interests in child protection and sudden infant death (the latter of which requires at least some understanding of both pathology and biochemistry).

The turning point in this journey, like its start, originated in Southeast Asia; this time, with a year spent with Servants to Asia's Urban Poor, working in a deprived area of Phnom Penh in the early 1990s. While there, I was confronted with poverty and suffering on a scale I hadn't encountered before. I saw first-hand the horrendous legacy of violence and war, and the ongoing injustice of corruption and exploitation of the poor. But I also saw signs of hope: the difference that individuals could make; the impact a small gesture of care can have; the transformation of people and communities that can occur when they are empowered to see and use their gifts and resources. That year in the slums of Cambodia also instilled in me, like never before, a deep questioning. I wanted to discover, to understand what lay behind these people's suffering; why there was so much violence and injustice; the pathways through which that

129

violence and injustice led to such devastating impacts on young children; and what we could do about it.

That year also led to both a questioning and a strengthening of my faith. Yes, I asked those hard questions of God: Why? Why this suffering? Why the injustice? Why haven't you done anything about it? I wasn't prepared to accept trite answers from narrow evangelical Christianity, nor from any other religious or secular philosophies. But through that, I am sure my faith has grown richer. Faith, of any sort, is not a matter of having simple answers to life's problems, but is an ongoing journey in which the questions and complaints are a vital part. And I could see, through fresh ways of exploring the life and teachings of Jesus, and the mystery of his death and resurrection, the seeds of a tangible hope reaching into these questions. Again, not in a simplistic (and, it increasingly seemed to me, selfish) concept of getting free entry to heaven when we die; but in the challenging, sacrificial path of getting alongside people in their suffering, and a life-long journey inspired by hope – the hope of a redeemed and renewed heaven and earth in which the injustice, violence, suffering and death that pervade our world will finally be no more.

Looking back, what I gave to Cambodia and its people during that year was minimal. I was young and inexperienced, we were only there short-term; I certainly made mistakes, and my attempts to learn the language and culture were, once again, woefully inadequate. But, as part of a team, we were there at the start of something quite incredible. One of my greatest joys has been to return to Cambodia over the ensuing years, and see the small team of our Cambodian co-workers – men and women we had recruited as translators and motorbike drivers, initially timid and disempowered – after years of persistent companionship by some of our fellow team members, grow to take the lead in a programme that expanded to touch the lives of thousands of individuals, families and communities in Phnom Penh; and eventually, many years later, to establish themselves as an autonomous Cambodian organisation.

While our part in that process was minimal, it was nevertheless real. And, at the same time, Cambodia gave to me a vision and a purpose that has grown to shape my subsequent journey in unexpected ways. That connection with poverty and suffering in Cambodia led me, on my return to the UK, to increasingly get involved in what I saw as some of the most needy areas of paediatrics, and to engage with some of the most vulnerable families in our country: those affected by disability, child abuse and neglect, and bereavement. The questioning that began during that year led to an ongoing questioning approach which led me into an academic career, seeing in research the opportunity to explore those questions in greater depth, and to seek to discover at least some answers along the way.

So there I was, 18 years later, a paediatrician engaging clinically with vulnerable children and families; taking a lead in child protection services both locally and nationally; and pursuing research to try to discover some of the root causes of child maltreatment and sudden infant death, and to learn how we can work to prevent such suffering. And along with that, learning how to be a father to my own children, seeking to engage with my teenage son, and jumping on a bicycle to accompany him on his incredible journey across the country. And then, unpredictably, having to take a back seat, submitting to a period of enforced rest, and learning to change gear and slow down.

The paediatrician learns to slow down

Surprisingly though, this wasn't nearly as hard as I thought it might be. Perhaps, in some way, this too was a continuation of a journey I had already started. While I enjoyed every aspect of my work, both clinical and academic, I didn't feel driven by it. I was happy to let bits go, to leave things to others while I took more of a back seat. As with our experience in Cambodia, I could appreciate that my greatest achievements may be in empowering others to take a lead, to achieve what they, and only they, could. My own responsibilities could wait – after all, no-one, least of all me, is indispensable. For now, I was content to be with Helen, to watch and encourage Joe as he completed his own challenge, and to enjoy all the other blessings of life and well-being.

I was still recovering. Even after the end of Joe's cycle ride, I found I got tired easily and physically had to slow down. In the background I continued to experience headaches – a necessary reminder, perhaps, that I couldn't expect to go back to my previous levels of activity and responsibility. But, at the same time, I had an incredible sense of well-being. And perhaps this is partly what the blessing sent to me by my Jewish friend tried to encapsulate: that health, or wholeness, is not simply dependent on being physically well. I was able to appreciate, more than ever before, the incredible blessing of having a loving family and friends. The hundreds of messages of love and concern from friends and colleagues across the country showed me, in a fresh way, just how important these relationships are. I was able to appreciate the renewal of old friendships, as we stayed with our friends Justin and Mary in Newcastle, and Andrew and Penny in Scotland; and to value a growing bond with Elizabeth, as she joined us again, following her mother's death, for the last two days of the ride.

For me, the highlight of the whole journey was probably the final Sunday evening, at Immervoulin campsite in the Trossachs. My parents had joined us for a couple of nights, and after a warming supper, we celebrated communion together: Helen and I, Joe, my Mum and Dad, and David. I was there, with my family, in the peace and beauty of the Scottish Highlands. Although Esther wasn't with us, I knew she was there in spirit, and that she had started her own exciting journey. And I was alive. And well. In that simple act of remembrance, I was able to feel an incredible sense of well-being; of shalom; of life in all its fullness.

CHAPTER 28

The Riders reach their destination

Therefore, since we are surrounded by such a great cloud of witnesses, let us throw off everything that hinders and the sin that so easily entangles, and let us run [cycle?] with perseverance the race marked out for us.
Hebrews 12 verse 1

Joe's Blog, 1st September:

After a very nice stay at Auchoyle House [with our friends Andrew and Penny], *we managed to set off at around half-nine. A rather grey and damp start as we headed on up the A9. I was very sore over the first few miles, but got better after a break, and some ibuprofen. Stopped for coffee and hot chocolate in a café at Bonar Bridge – the first time over the whole ride that the coffee has been cheaper.*

After a brief stop, Joe and David cycled on through Lairg, then 13 miles up over the moor towards Crask Inn. This amazing, isolated inn is situated at 230 metres above sea level, in the middle of the Highland moors, and surrounded by... nothing. We all stopped there and celebrated with a glass of malt whisky. The proprietor came out to chat with us, and told us of another unicyclist who had stayed there 13 years ago near the start of a John O'Groats to Land's End ride on a standard 20-inch unicycle. I had feared that this would prove to be a hard ride, but the gradient was incredibly gentle, so although climbing high, the team made it with ease, and were rewarded with one of the finest day's rides in the whole journey, surrounded by spectacular Highland scenery, grasslands, mountains and sheep. I was pleased with my route planning having taken them this way, and once again, felt a tinge of sadness that I was not cycling with them on this penultimate stretch.

A wee dram to celebrate at the Crask Inn

Joe's audio diary:

We're just outside the Crask Inn now, and I had my first taste of whisky (disgusting). I've just noticed that there's another one of the Royal Bank of Scotland signposts. I think there were two a few days ago; no idea what that brings the total to, but never mind. It's been a very nice day of riding on the whole; uphill all the way from Lairg, but fairly gentle, and, according to this signpost, John O'Groats is 90 miles. It's about 85 according to our route, but anyway. Thirty-five more miles today, then only one day left. Very nice scenery round here.

As I said, very nice scenery around here. Big areas of grass with a few rivers running through it; reminding me rather a lot of when we visited 'Edoras' in New Zealand. [A few years ago, we had spent a family holiday visiting family and friends in New Zealand. Being great Tolkien fans, we had taken the opportunity to visit a few of the filming sites for the *Lord of the Rings* movies, including a magnificent day, in the wilds of the South Island, miles from anywhere, where they had recreated Edoras in Rohan.] *Slight change now, in that I've just passed a whole forest being cut down, or what looks like it: huge piles of logs going for quite a long way up the hill actually; also got passed by a timber lorry, which may well have been carrying logs from here. Possibly my least favourite type of vehicle; we've had a few of them in Scotland, and it isn't too much fun having one going past you.*

And back to the 'Edoras' kind of countryside. The sun's come out, and what looks rather like a slight tail-wind. On the whole the road is very quiet. A bit up and down, but not too bad.

In the middle of nowhere – the two cyclists in the Scottish Highlands

You know that feeling you get at the end of a really, really long cycle ride? Or near the end anyway, when you're just getting more and more tired, and you're starting to feel really sore, and you just can't wait to get to the end? I haven't got it.

A huge number of deer away to my right now.

In keeping with all the Edoras-ish scenery around here, I've just passed a sign to Helmsdale: not quite Helm's Deep, but close enough.

Riding along next to a loch now [Loch Naver]. *Just under 60 miles so far today, so only 20 left. And the sun's just gone behind a cloud. How mean of it.*

A very cool bridge over the river just to my right here. If I had more time I'd go over it, but obviously I haven't. This obviously being the same river that I've been following for well over 10 miles now actually, and I imagine we'll be following it pretty much all the way down to the coast. I say down, it seems to go uphill half the time which is interesting, considering the fact that it's a river, but oh well. I've just had a nice conversation with a passing motorcyclist, who's doing a bit of touring around Scotland and was very impressed by the unicycle. Somewhere in the region of 10 more miles now today, so will probably have a bit of a break soon. David's somewhere ahead. It's quarter past five, so making pretty good time on the whole. It's been a very nice day.

Just passed the turning to Helmsdale, and there's a horse looking suspiciously like a fat version of Shadowfax over there.

My progress over the past 10 miles will be largely due to two of mankind's greatest inventions: the wheel, and the Jelly Baby.

David managed to reach the junction 45 minutes ahead of me. He's had an average speed of 14½ miles an hour for the whole day, which actually is probably close to my top speed to be honest. It's rather nicely summed up by the poster at the side of the road, which says, 'Woah Dave!' Not too far to the campsite now. And then 50 miles tomorrow. Oh yes.

As they set out the following morning from our final campsite at Bettyhill, I sensed a slight degree of nervous anticipation in Joe. Having come this far, and with all they'd been through, he was determined to get to the end. As quickly as he could. He and David pushed off, and Joe set a cracking pace, hardly stopping at all for the whole 50 miles. Their route took them along the A836 hugging the North Scotland coast, past the massive Dounreay power station and through Thurso and on. Across the sea to the north, the cliffs of the Orkney Islands crept into view, alternately bathed in sun, then drenched in spectacular sheets of rain. Joe didn't waver at all, keeping up a steady 12-13 mph for the full 52 miles.

Joe's final Blog, Friday 2nd September, 2011:

And we'd finished. I achieved a top speed of 21.5 mph coming in to John O'Groats, and an average speed of 12.1 over the day. We crossed the 'line' at 1:51 pm. It has taken us 18 days, 22 hours and 51 minutes to travel the 1,200 miles from Land's End.

Success – the whole team at John O'Groats

As they cycled down the last stretch of road into John O'Groats and over our makeshift finishing line, I couldn't help feeling a tremendous sense of pride and achievement. It wasn't just Joe and David who were finishing this incredible quest. I too was a part of it, as were Helen and Elizabeth, and all those countless people who had helped and encouraged us along the way. The writer of the epistle to the Hebrews talks of a great cloud of witnesses, urging us along in the race, relating this to those men and women of faith who have gone before. It seemed to me that, as David and Joe pressed on over those final miles and raced to the end in John O'Groats, a great cloud of witnesses was watching them all the way: friends and family across this country urging them on to complete this quest; people who themselves had been inspired by the courage and commitment of a young unicyclist, and his companions on the road.

And a glass of champagne to celebrate!

Epilogue

The ride complete, Joe was focusing, once again, on freestyle unicycling; squeezing it in among the competing demands of A-levels, drama, other circus skills, and playing the tenor horn in a wind band. And where does all this lead? What does a long-distance unicyclist do, once he's completed Lejog?

Essentially, ever since I began this ride, the question I have been asked most (excluding 'lost a wheel?') is 'what's next?' Or words to that effect. Many people seem to have an idea that, having ridden from Land's End to John O'Groats, I will embark on an even greater adventure sometime soon. Suggestions have been made. The most common one was coast to coast across America, though it's been concluded that that's not too much fun. Nicer rides have also been suggested, mainly in Europe.

There's no shortage of rides out there. But I'm going to state here that I'm not intending to do another big ride anytime soon. I'm starting A-levels, I've got a busy year ahead, and I wouldn't mind a bit of free time next summer holidays. So I'm going to put the big wheel aside for a while. I would like to do another ride, sometime in the future. But it won't be for a very long time. Certainly not in the next two years.

Be warned, though. The day will come when I hit the road again. It will probably be on a geared unicycle. It will probably be for a long time. It will probably be without a support car. And most importantly... it will be Epic.

In the hours and days following our completion of the ride, hundreds of texts, email and Facebook messages and blog comments came pouring in, congratulating Joe and David on their success, and expressing people's admiration and love for all of us. And the sponsorship, already well exceeding our initial target of £6,000, rose to phenomenal levels as many more people gave so generously to support the three charities. In the end, we raised over £13,000 for charity, which in itself was an exciting achievement, and seemed to capture the spirit of generosity, hope and inspiration that we had set out for.

We all owe a tremendous debt of gratitude to all those who gave. Without their inspiration and encouragement I'm not sure it would have been possible for Joe and David to keep going so faithfully. It is, of course, impossible to thank everyone who has given, but suffice it to say that each person, in their own way, has been an inspiration and encouragement to us all. I shall leave the last words to Joe, the unicyclist who of course was the inspiration and motivation for this whole, mad, exciting venture...

Thank you.

Firstly, to the support team, especially Mum, who worked incredibly hard to keep me and David going.

To David, for accompanying me on the ride, and carrying most of the baggage.

To all the other companions who have joined us on various stages of the route:

- *Mark, in Cornwall.*
- *Brian, our guide through Bristol.*
- *Jeremy, who joined us for parts of the days either side of Coventry.*
- *All the police who joined us through Warwick.*
- *Rachel, who rode the last few miles into Coventry with us.*
- *All the HTC cyclists who joined us when we left Cov.*
- *Roger, who unicycled into Durham with us.*
- *Justin, who guided me through Newcastle.*
- *Jane, who joined us for two days after Newcastle.*
- *Wendy, who joined us out of Morpeth, and John, who rode with us for an hour that day.*
- *The Doggetts, who were great company for two days in Scotland.*
- *To all the people who we stayed with – Brian and Edwina in Bristol; Justin and Mary in Newcastle, and the Evenetts in Scotland.*
- *To everybody who has been following the blog, praying, and encouraging us.*

- *To the hundreds of people who have sponsored us.*
- *To all the random people who encouraged us along the way, or gave us directions when we were lost.*
- *And finally, Dad. This ride would not have happened without him.*

Postscript

Five months after the conclusion of that epic journey, our lives were once again turned upside down. Helen, the person who had really kept us going through it all, died unexpectedly of a heart attack. She was on her way home from a two-week trip to the Philippines with Servants when she collapsed at Manila airport.

Helen's death left a huge hole in all of our lives, and left us, once again, wondering how we could go on, pick up the pieces and begin again a new and different journey. While we all feel the immense pain of her loss, we can also look back with gratitude on so many happy memories – of the fun, the struggles and the love we have all shared over the years; and we are encouraged by the love of so many, here in the UK and around the world, who have themselves been touched by Helen's life, her tireless work for Servants, and the love she showed to all she met.

The months leading up to her death had been hard ones for Helen. Not least, the strain of organising and seeing this trip through to completion, and the stress of my own illness. During her two weeks in Manila, however, she had discovered, in an incredibly powerful way, a real sense of peace.

Are you tired? Worn out? Burned out on religion? Come to me. Get away with me and you'll recover your life. I'll show you how to take a real rest. Walk with me and work with me – watch how I do it. Learn the unforced rhythms of grace. I won't lay anything heavy or ill-fitting on you. Keep company with me and you'll learn to live freely and lightly.
(Matthew 11: 28-30, The Message)